January 1987
with love,
Agi.

JULIE STAFFORD

TASTE OF LIFE

FOR CHILDREN

Greenhouse

For Timothy and Cassie
Wishing you health and happiness.

Very little is needed to make a happy, healthy life. It is all within yourself, in your way of thinking and eating.

First published in 1986 by
Greenhouse Publications Pty Ltd
385 Bridge Road
Richmond 3121
Victoria Australia

Typeset by Abb-typesetting Pty Ltd, Melbourne,
from wordprocessed computer disks
by Dead-Set Publishing Services, Melbourne

Printed and bound by Kyodo-Shing Loong, Singapore

Cover design by Warwick Cruise
Photography by Phil Wymant, Latrobe Studios

ISBN 0 86436 0 30 4

Distributed by Gordon & Gotch (Australia) Limited
Melbourne, Sydney, Brisbane, Perth, Adelaide

Distributed by Gordon & Gotch (NZ) Ltd
Auckland, Wellington, Christchurch

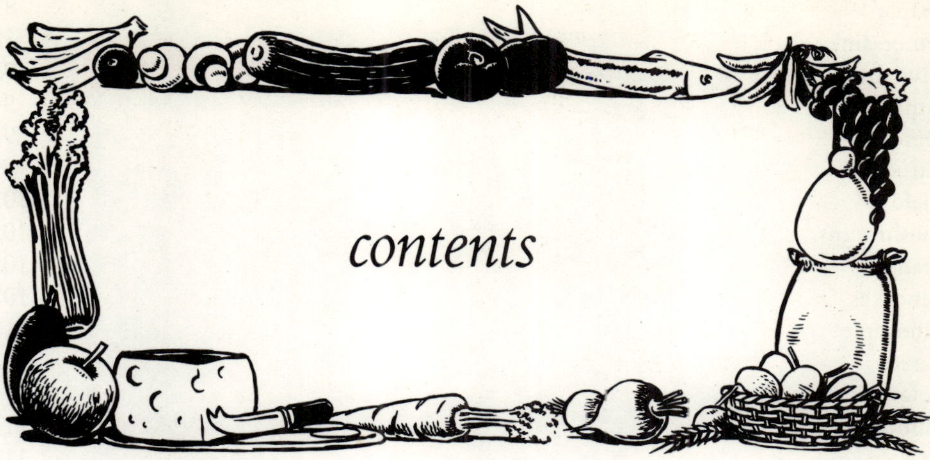

contents

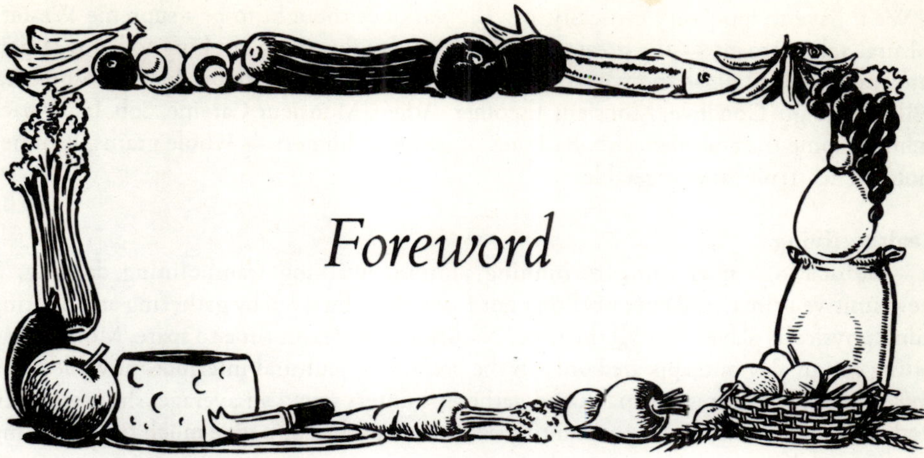

Foreword

How we eat now

Until about 200 years ago, only the rich had much chance of regularly filling up on energy dense, concentrated or refined nutrients. But today, in the Western consumers' world of butter and eggs and sugar and steak, we can all get, all the time and with little physical effort, all the sweet, and the soft and the savoury and the smooth foods we want, and that is far more than we need, physiologically — so our bodies store the excess. We become overweight.

I am pointing out to you again the magnitude and simplicity of this current Western nutritional situation, because the stark medical facts about it are only just beginning to dawn on everyone in a national way. As a direct result of the modes in which we in the Western world now eat energy dense and fibre poor foods and take little exercise, about one-third of our population is becoming sick. Most of our bowel trouble, stomach trouble, heart trouble, artery trouble, blood pressure, strokes, diabetes, obesity and premature death come from this one cause. The total burden of disablement is hard to assess, but it is something like a third of the people being less effective, of requiring care or actually dying.

The price of haute cuisine

It seems that little or none of this disability is inevitable. It seems that if we could apply the commonsense we now have concerning eating and exercising we would as a whole people become more effective in this new technical environment which we have created.

That was the sort of biological leap forward we made when we conquered the infectious diseases a century ago. It looks as though we have another such job before us now. The saving in terms of national effectiveness will be billions and billions of dollars. The gain in sheer happiness will be enormous through the elimination of vast amounts of sickness, disability and discomfort. Politicians, opinion leaders, doctors and all whose duties are forward looking and concerned with national welfare and economy of effort should concern themselves with this feeding problem. It's just that our modern eating needs a few little adjustments. No one wants to discard the advantages of technical civilisation. We have only to eliminate one of its disadvantages.

First, let us all get a good understanding of our own biological history as a species, particularly in relation to what we eat. We cannot get rid of eating, it is a human good. But relying on our in-built instincts to guide us has pushed us into consumer preference situations that, satisfied and persisted with year after year, are driving us into this public health problem.

We'll have to look very critically at what was once thought to be a supreme Western cultural achievement — the great cuisine of Europe. European cooking today is largely based on meat and sugar and white flour and animal fats and dairy products. Most of that will have to go. Goodbye, Monsieur Escoffier. Adieu, Monsieur Careme. Sob. In, or back in, must come the complex carbohydrates of gatherer-hunters — whole grains, legumes, roots, stems, fruits and vegetables.

Healthy living

In — or back in — must come the running, jumping, walking, trampolining, dancing, of the primitive primates. Remember that our forebears who lived by gathering and hunting didn't physically slave away all the time. Nature always leaves time to spare. Moiling and toiling day in, day out, appeared only in the peasant agricultural interlude, now blessedly over in the West. Forest primates and gatherer-hunters spend an average, short while in moderately athletic gathering or hunting each day, but they also give much time to lazing around, socialising.

Socialising is, of course, also an important aspect of eating. The meal time is a vital get-together, an essential human ritual. When a primate gatherer-hunter — and I'm calling them that rather than hunter-gatherers because they did much more gathering than hunting — brought back a gathering or a catch to the group there was a sharing of the food.

This regular sharing, along with the suckling relationship between mother and child, has been a basic bond forming ritual knitting human society together. It goes very deep. We constantly use it. The business lunch. The lovers' supper. The family dinner where the male hunter at one end of the table ritually dismembers a successfully hunted roast animal with a greatly oversized carving knife, while the female gatherer ritually 'helps' (as we say) everyone to her successfully gathered vegetables.

Whatever we eat, we will still need meal times, and also, when we feel like it, we will still need to feast, to feel full. I don't see why all that shouldn't continue. I don't see any need for miserable 'dieting'. I don't see why we cannot feast on complex carbohydrates, on the new dishes made from grains, beans and vegetables. We can still have some meat and fat and sugar, but much less than we do now.

We will, of course, need clever cooks to work on the new dishes and make them marvellous. We'll need much better wholegrain breads. We'll still need fast foods, so steaming or microwave heating will have to replace the energy dense boiling oil into which at present we plunge nearly everything we want to heat or cook quickly for people on the move.

I would think that with exercise, and without the sweet, fat, energy stuffed foods, we will retain healthy guts and healthy arteries. Strokes and coronaries will disappear and we'll all lose or gain weight — but mostly lose it — until we are whatever natural size our personal genetic programming means us to be.

Mind you, there are great farming, catering, industrial, and retailing interests that will have to adjust themselves to all this. But they'll do it, slowly and steadily, in response to what I think is certain to be the changing Western market for food, simply because of the growing knowledge of what certain foods do to you.

In the long run, Western peoples will prefer not to be digging their graves with their teeth. Having been first into solving the civilised ecological problem of infectious disease, they will also be first into solving the social-industrial problem of paradoxical overnutrition.

Earle Hackett, M.D. Norton Summit, SA

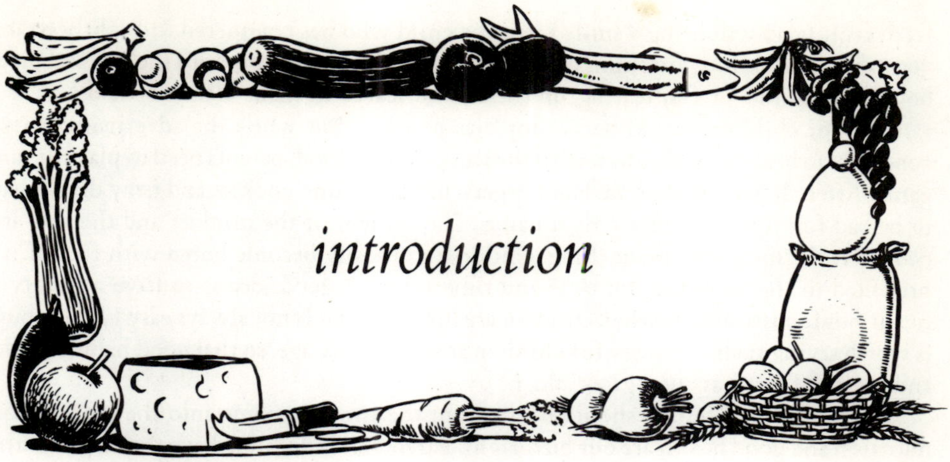

introduction

Where do you start to write a cookbook for children when the tastes of childhood are so vast and varied? I know children who at the age of three have been the greatest connoisseurs of vintage cheeses, olives, salamis, the richest of desserts and the hottest of curries. I also know some teenagers who will only eat peanut butter sandwiches and when served a salad or cooked vegetables with the main meat meal, quickly turn up their noses and move the vegetables to the furthest edge of their dinner plate. Some have even been known to pocket the vegetables and discard them to the house pet later. Who said children were no longer innovative? These children shall remain nameless. Parents scream and pull their hair out. Where did we go wrong? Perhaps we fussed too much in an attempt to win praise in the kitchen, to have our children complete three meals a day or to have scrap free plates at the end of a meal. Somewhere in there we forgot not to worry. Children, after all, have never been known to starve themselves for too long.

The earlier that children become involved and participate in the preparing of nutritious foods, the quicker they will develop an understanding about the variety of foods available and the value of this nutritious food for their bodies. Children should be taught as they grow that food is a source of energy that operates their bodies. It is the fuel that feeds the machine. They then have the opportunity to accept the responsibility for their own health and have the knowledge to make sensible decisions about what they actually put in their mouths every day.

As young children are introduced to solids, meal times can be a play time for exploring foods of different colours, textures, shapes and flavours. As young children begin to play with food, the most natural thing for them to do is to put their fingers into their mouths. In this way they are introduced to different flavours. At this age, the easiest meal to prepare for small children is a bits and pieces bowl. This can include variations of the following ingredients: raw diced vegetables and fruits, small pieces of wholemeal bread, a spoonful of brown cooked rice and other cooked grains or beans. If cooking any of the vegetables and fruits, do not disguise them by mashing them together or by adding butter, sugar or salt. Let children discover the natural flavour of foods, and when buying tinned or packaged food, make sure it is not 100 per cent refined and that it is free of salt, sugar and preservatives.

Children will appreciate the opportunity to work with you in the kitchen, exploring the colours, textures and shapes of foods. By cutting, tearing, shredding and dicing foods, the presentation of food can be changed over and over again to maintain interest and enjoyment. As soon as children are able to sit on a stool at a bench, or in a high chair, and can use a blunt knife, let them participate in cooking activities. For instance, mastering a fresh fruit salad will bring a smile from the child who has conquered it! Lightly cooked vegetables like carrots, zucchini, potatoes, etc. can be cut up to put into the bits and pieces bowl and it's lots of fun tearing up the lettuce leaves to make a tossed salad!

Food for children should be as simple as possible. But while the advertising market continues to brainwash children with the value of junk food, parents need to play the same game. After all, who said pizza, hamburgers, fish and chips, cookies and fizzy drinks have to be bad for you? They are only a name. The content of the product and the way it is cooked is the most important thing. Children can easily become bored with food if it is presented in the same fashion time and time again. A good idea is to have a variety of nutritious foods available when children are hungry. This is not always easy I know, but it is worth trying such a strategy for children at a very early age, so that good habits develop and are reinforced as they grow older.

A good dietary lifestyle should begin from the time we come into the world. Good nutrition and good health are our birthright. Parents and educators have the responsibility to make sure children have the opportunity to discover, to understand and to participate in good nutrition and be rewarded with good health.

The diseases of our affluent Western society like heart disease, cancer, diabetes, obesity and others are partly, if not wholly, caused by a high fat, high protein, salt loaded, sugar loaded, high refined foods diet. Omitting these foods from the diet will not necessarily mean you and your family will be free from any disease in your whole lifetime. But prevention is better than cure, and the quality of your life will be greatly enhanced by omitting them.

Deaths from heart disease, diabetes and cancer are increasing in Western societies at an alarming rate.

Deaths from	Australia 1982		America 1982		United Kingdom 1982	
	Number	Percentage of total deaths	Number	Percentage of total deaths	Number	Percentage of total deaths
Heart Disease	38,786	33.8	731,708	37.1	189,768	32.6
Cancers	24,914	21.7	433,795	22.0	130,561	22.4
Diabeties	1,609	1.4	34,583	2.8	4,534	0.8
Deaths caused	65,309	56.9	1,200,086	60.8	324,933	55.8

Obesity is also a major problem for the affluent nations. Estimates of its prevalence range from 10–50 per cent or more of the adult population. ('International symposia on nutrition and obesity', *Medical Journal of Australia*, 1 April 1985.) Established obesity in childhood is highly resistant to treatment in the long term. Up to 80 per cent of fat young children become fat older children and adults. (Court, J. M., 'The development of obesity in childhood', *Medical Journal of Australia*, 1979.)

The years of childhood are the learning years, the informative years, years of exploration. They are years that pass all too quickly. They undoubtedly should be years to develop a 'Taste of life'.

Good health,

Julie Stafford

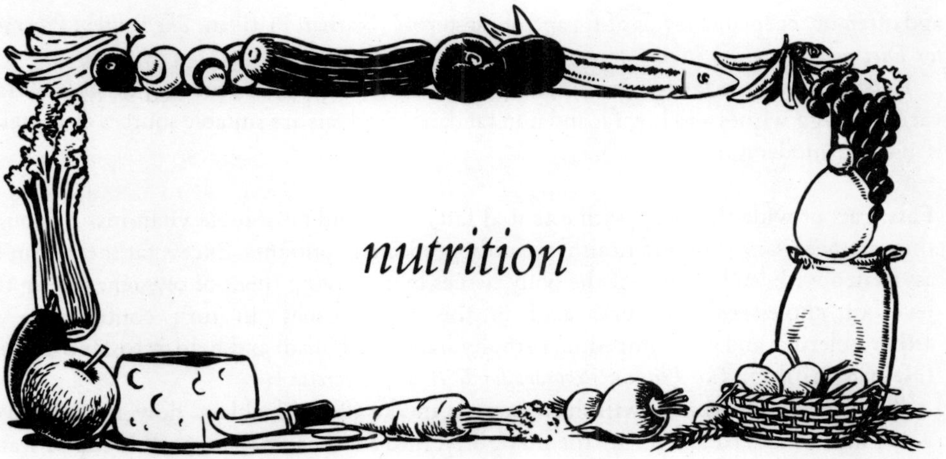

nutrition

Nutrition sustains the body. The food we eat utilises the energy it provides; it is the fuel that operates the machine. Good nutrition depends on how wisely we choose the food we eat. A combination of complex carbohydrates, proteins, fats, vitamins and minerals is essential and should be provided by our diet.

Complex carbohydrates: These are the body's source of energy. Sugar is perhaps the most commonly known carbohydrate but it is a refined carbohydrate with more harmful than beneficial effects. Refined, it is stripped of its fibre and nutritional value. Sugar includes sucrose (table sugar), lactose (milk sugar), fructose (fruit sugar), honey and glucose. The average Australian consumes sugar in excess — at least one kilogram of sugar per week. Excess sugar in the diet can be directly linked with obesity, diabetes, hypertension, hypoglycemia and artherosclerosis (an early sign of heart disease). It provides a lot of calories with few nutrients.

Unrefined carbohydrates or complex carbohydrates which include the starch rich natural foods like grains, roots, vegetables and fruits, are an excellent source of energy.

The body takes longer to break down complex carbohydrates. Therefore it can tolerate the level of glucose being absorbed into the bloodstream at the one time. Another bonus with complex carbohydrates is that they contain essential fibre which is beneficial for good health. When fibre is lacking from the diet, health problems like constipation, haemorrhoids, appendicitis, hiatus hernia and colon cancer are evident. A recent study (Duncan, 1980) of 400 4-year-olds in the La Trobe Valley, Victoria, showed that 12 per cent were severely constipated!

In the early twentieth century modern technology provided machines to refine a lot of foods. It enabled us to create the six inch high sponge filled with cream, the three inch high scones to serve with jam and cream, the French croissant to fill with ham and cheese, the snowiest of white bread and so on. The shelves of bakehouses never looked so good, but we forgot that food nutrients are an essential part of survival. In many cases we have milled the goodness out of the food, leaving a visual delight but a nutrition lacking disaster.

Proteins: The body requires protein to build new cells and repair damaged tissues, and to help maintain body tissues. 'Grains, roots, vegetables and fruits in an unrefined, minimally processed form are an excellent source of protein. These foods are a much better source of protein than animal foods such as meat, fish, eggs and milk which usually have very high and often unacceptable levels of fat and cholesterol.' (Nathan Pritikin, *The Pritikin Program for Diet and Exercise.*)

Red meat (visible fat removed), chicken (skin and visible fat removed), fish (low fat varieties), egg whites and low fat and non fat dairy products are suitable sources of protein if used in moderation.

Fats: Fats provide the body with essential fatty acids and fat soluble vitamins. Although they are necessary for good health, we only need small amounts. Excess fat intake can be associated with 'suffocation of the body tissues by depriving them of oxygen; raising the level of cholesterol and uric acid in the body tissues, in turn contributing to artherosclerosis and gout; impeding carbohydrate metabolism and help to foster diabetes.' (Nathan Pritikin, *The Pritikin Program for Diet and Exercise.*)

This simple experiment will show how fat intake affects the blood flow. Pour a cup of water into a small jar and secure the lid tightly. Into another small jar pour ¾ cup of water and add ¼ cup of liquid oil. Secure tightly with a lid. Shake both bottles. Notice how the jar with the oil is more sluggish and heavier in its movements. The liquid slides on the inside walls of the jar. This is similar to what happens when we eat a meal high in fats. The fat in the bloodstream makes the flow of blood sluggish and slower.

Depending on how much fat has already built up in our blood carrying vessels (arteries, capillaries), fat adheres to and builds up on the walls of these vessels creating a substance called plaque. Oxygen flow is restricted and, under stress, stroke and heart attack are possible. Continued excess fat in the diet can eventually lead to blockage of the blood carrying vessels and heart attack is almost guaranteed.

Although fat is the most concentrated form of energy, taken in excess it is a retarding form of energy, and it is more beneficial to obtain energy from complex carbohydrates. Moderation of the intake of all fats is essential for good health.

Vitamins: Vitamins are organic substances, present in small amounts in different foods. They cannot be produced by the body, so they need to be absorbed from a varied diet. There are at least thirteen essential vitamins required by the body to function effectively and for normal growth.

The fat soluble vitamins are A, D, E and K. These are not soluble in water and can be stored in the body to be used as required.

The water soluble vitamins are B_1 (thiamin), B_2 (riboflavin), B_6, B_{12} (only a very small amount required), biotin, folic acid, pantothenic acid and vitamin C (ascorbic acid). These are soluble in water and cannot be stored by the body. Surplus amounts are readily washed from the body in urine and perspiration. If taken in supplement form in excess quantities they can have a toxic effect on the body. A diet which includes a variety of fresh and lightly cooked foods offers the best source of vitamins.

Minerals: Minerals are inorganic substances also needed by the body for growth and good nutrition. There are at least fifteen important minerals needed in our diet. These include sodium, potassium, chlorine, calcium, magnesium, phosphorus, sulphur, chromium, copper, iodine, manganese, molybdenum, selenium and zinc. Again, a well balanced diet will include these essential minerals without the need to supplement your diet.

Supplementing your diet with vitamins or minerals may be necessary in extreme situations, under excess stress or when the body is ailing, but it should only be done under the supervision of an experienced person, i.e. a medical practitioner or naturopath.

Fibre: Fibre's function is to create bulk in the intestine and move faeces through the system quickly to avoid the build-up of toxins in the body. Excess fibre in the diet can interfere with the absorption of some minerals and vitamins. Some recipes in this book have taken into account the amount of fibre in a given recipe and have been regulated accordingly (cakes, cookies, breads, muffins, etc.). Unbleached, chemical free. preservative free flour has been added to some of these recipes to reduce the possibility of excessive fibre for children.

Water: Water is just as essential as other nutrients, if not more essential. The body requires anywhere between four and eight glasses of water per day so that it can effectively carry out its bodily functions. Water helps to provide a means of transport for nutrients to be carried through the body, and for wastes and toxins to be expelled from the body. Water also helps to maintain body temperature.

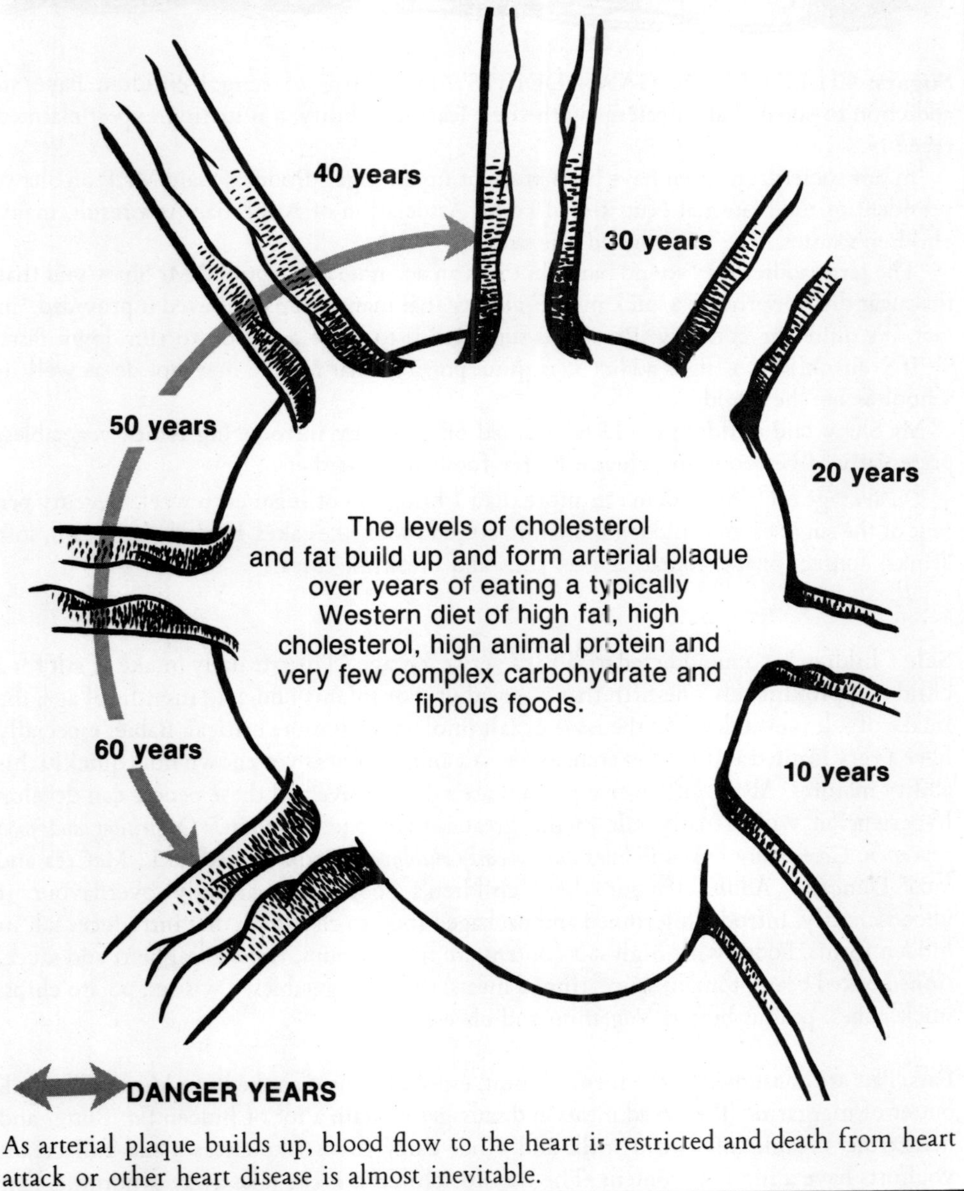

As arterial plaque builds up, blood flow to the heart is restricted and death from heart attack or other heart disease is almost inevitable.

addictive foods

Sugars: CHILDREN 'SUGAR ADDICTS'. Two-thirds of school children have an addiction to sugar that interferes with their learning ability, a nutrition expert claimed recently.

'In our society, children have been brought up on sugar products', said Mr Ron Shaw, president of the National Nutritional Foods Association of Australia. 'As a result, many children's tastes have been dulled', he said.

'The term addict may sound harsh but it is an accurate description.' Mr Shaw said that the sugar did not provide a 'pick me up' quality that many people believed it provided. 'In fact, it's quite the contrary. Processed sugar tends to cause a person to run down fast.

'If your child is a sugar addict it is quite possible that he/she may not do as well in school as he/she could.'

Mr Shaw said children could be weaned off sugar by introducing fruits, vegetables, preservative free foods and chemical free foods to their diets.

On average each Australian eats more than 1 kilogram of sugar each week. Seventy per cent of the sugar eaten is hidden in manufactured foods like cakes, biscuits, ice cream, soft drinks, confectionary, tomato sauce, jams and breakfast cereals.

Salt: Children become addicted to salt at a very early age. 'The safe daily intake of salt for a child is approximately one-fifth that of an adult. For infants under 12 months of age, the intake of salt is even less and the issue of salt intolerance is more critical. Babies especially have a very limited ability to excrete excess salt and it is not as yet known how quickly this ability matures. About one in five persons are salt sensitive and these people can develop hypertension with a daily salt intake greater than one teaspoon.' (*Nutrition and food education: Community responsibilities during early childhood*, Book 3, Nadine L. McCrea and Suzi Duncan.) Adults flavour their children's food and naturally overflavour it unconsciously. Introducing tinned and packaged food to children's diet introduces salt in hidden forms. Foods with high salt content are tinned soups, tinned spaghetti and sauce, tinned baked beans, tomato sauce, tinned meats, tinned vegetables, Twisties, potato chips, stock cubes, peanut butter, Vegemite and cheeses.

Fats: Fats are consumed in the form of meat, especially meat cooked in additional fat, oil, butter or margarine. Preserved meats and sausages contain a lot of hidden fat. Butter and margarine, cream, full cream milk and other dairy foods like cheeses and full cream yoghurts have a high fat content. The trap for children is the take-away syndrome. Fast foods (better known as junk foods) like fish and chips, hamburgers, pizza, deep fried foods and ice cream have unknown fat quantities as well as hidden salt and sugar.

Preservatives and artificial colours and flavours: These are found in most refined, packaged and tinned foods. Many have been removed from foods as they have been found to be harmful to the body. There is some thought that they may be linked to hyperactivity in children and cause allergy like reactions.

Caffeine: 'Caffeine is a drug known to produce peculiar and rapid heart beats, insomnia, high free fatty acid levels in the blood, high blood glucose levels in diabetics, increased gastric acid secretions and high blood pressure.' (Nathan Pritikin, *The Pritikin Program for Diet and Exercise.*) Children unknowingly consume large quantities of caffeine in chocolate, cocoa and cola drinks. A small chocolate bar contains approximately 25mg of caffeine. A glass of Coca Cola contains approximately 40mg. 'Consider this: A 7-year-old boy who drinks three Cokes a day — since he weighs about 60lbs — is actually drinking the equivalent of eight cups of coffee that a 175lb man would drink.' (Nathan Pritikin)

dos and don'ts

Do

- Accept that healthy children do not starve themselves to death through food refusal.
- Accept that appetite determines how much a child will eat. If the child is not hungry, the child does not need to eat.
- Leave food in view of the child for a set time. Then remove the food. Uneaten food can be eaten at the next meal time. Seal it and keep it refrigerated. Develop a consistent pattern such as a bell ringing to indicate the start and finish of meal times.
- Teach children about nutrition at an early age.
- Encourage them to participate in food preparation.
- Encourage children to drink plenty of water, rather than sugar diluted juices, cordials or fizzy drinks, to wash out the wastes and toxins in their system which is a natural process of digestion.
- Encourage their involvement by creating a small vegetable and herb patch that they can help maintain and collect produce from.
- Encourage them to become label readers and to distinguish between necessary additives and unnecessary additives.
- Involve them in the shopping experience. It is a good time to teach them to be selective in their food choice, especially with fruits and vegetables. Buy these in season when they are cheaper and more nutritious. Bruised, wilted and pale coloured fruits and vegetables are not fresh.
- Teach children to avoid and overcome stress at an early age. A state of relaxed calm is easily achieved by teaching your child to breathe deeply, through the nose and from the abdomen in long, slow breaths.
- Encourage children to be active and participate in outdoor exercises. Walking and deep breathing in the fresh air is probably the easiest and the best way.
- Teach children that feeling good and looking good are a result of eating good food — *we are what we eat.*

Don't

- Have adult expectations of how much a child should eat.
- Use food as a reward or a punishment (for obvious reasons).
- Offer food to children between meals if they do not eat food at meal times.
- Expect children to eat nutritious food if the cupboards are full of other foods and the adults in the house only eat these foods. Children will naturally copy adult behaviour.

How to avoid degenerative disease

Eat well. The human body must be the greatest machine of all. It is a delicate system of connected pipes and organs which, when fed the proper quality and quantity of fuel, perform the most extraordinary tasks. High quality food allows the human body to work most effectively.

Exercise well. Exercising develops healthy muscles and tissues and ensures better blood circulation and an adequate flow of oxygen to vital organs. This provides increased energy and stamina, increased flexibility, co-ordination and body control. Exercises also make you feel great!

Rest well. The body needs sleep and quiet times to regenerate energy.

Diseases of an affluent world and their associated problems
Why we need to reduce cholesterol and fat

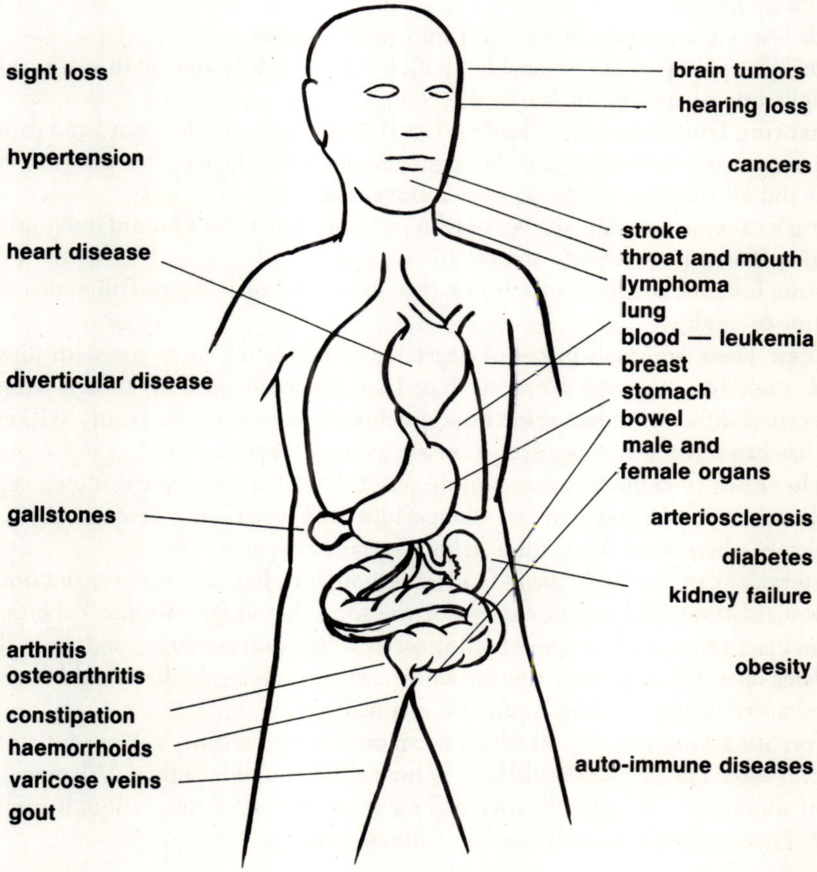

This diagram shows the diseases which are considered to be linked with a diet of high fat, high cholesterol, high protein, high salt, high sugar, refined foods, added preservatives and food colourings.

cooking terms

Lightly grease: If greasing is necessary, use a good quality cold compressed oil (olive oil). Lightly wipe over the surface of the cookware and wipe off any excess using a tissue. This technique will protect the surface of the cookware and food will not stick. Most cookware will not need to be washed. Wipe over with oil while still hot and remove any small particles of food.
Diced: Use a sharp knife to cut food into small squares.
Shred: This applies to leafy vegetables. Roll leaves up tightly and cut thinly or thickly in a straight line to the end of leaves.
Segmenting fruit: Use a sharp knife. Place the fruit upright on a board and pare off the peel and pith in even slices. Cut the segments out individually after the fruit has been peeled and all traces of white pith have been removed.
Testing a cake: Insert a fine skewer or thin piece of straw from a broom into the centre of the cake. If it comes out dry, the cake is cooked.
Julienne: Julienne strips are matchstick thin pieces of vegetables or fruits such as carrot, zucchini or apple.
Crudites: These are small pieces of vegetable to nibble on, or to use with dips.
Puree: Place food through a fine sieve or food processor until all food is smooth.
Serves: It is difficult to determine how much each person in the family will eat. This book has based the serves per recipe on an 'average' appetite.
Blanche: Place food quickly into boiling water, leave for just a few minutes, depending on what the food is, and remove. Plunge into iced water for a few moments to cool completely, then drain. Blanching helps to retain crispness.
Simmer: Cook on low heat. Bring food to the boil, turn heat down, cover and simmer for the required time. The liquid content of the food should be only just bubbling.
Steam: Place food on a rack above boiling water. The steam penetrates and cooks the food, but water does not come into contact with it. Hence, nutrients that would normally be washed away in the cooking liquid are retained.
Stir fry: Stir frying without oil or stock can only be successfully achieved if a non stick surface is used. The surface should be very hot before you add the food. When you add the food it should be continuously stirred for a short period of time. Liquids can then be added. This method is mainly used in Chinese cooking.

measurements and oven temperatures

1 metric cup = 250ml
1 tablespoon = 20ml
1 teaspoon = 5ml
Spoon measures are level measurements.

Slow oven	150–170°C	300-350°F
Moderate oven	170–190°C	350–375°F
Hot oven	200°C	400°F
Very hot oven	220-240°C	425–450°F

Conversions and substitutes:

¼ teaspoon dried herbs = 2 tablespoons fresh herbs
2 cloves fresh garlic crushed = 1 teaspoon powdered garlic
4 teaspoons dry yeast = 30g fresh yeast
1 cup carob powder = ¾ cup cocoa powder
2½ medium sized lemon = ½ cup lemon juice
1 medium sized onion = approximately 100g
1 cup uncooked brown rice = nearly 3 cups cooked brown rice
2 cups uncooked soyaroni noodles = 3 cups cooked noodles
1 cup skim milk powder = 4 cups liquid milk
1 cup wholemeal flour = approximately 150g
1 cup rolled oats = approximately 150g
1 cup whole almonds = approximately 150g
1 teaspoon agar powder will set approximately 1¼–2 cups of liquid, depending on setting consistency required.
1x26cm agar bar will set approximately 3 cups of liquid.

overleaf: Julie and Bruce Stafford with Timothy and Cassie, all helping to prepare a meal

opposite: Fun food with apple and cheese kebabs (page 28), cucumber pots (page 69), cucumber boats (page 69), and strawberry caterpillar (page 130)

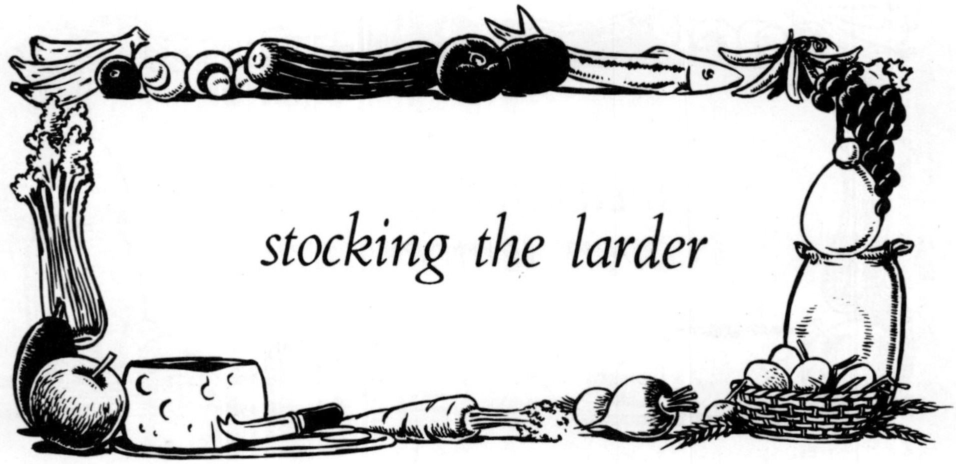

stocking the larder

Almonds: These are the only nuts used in the recipes. Although almonds have a high fat content, they are a high quality, nutritious food. However, to reduce fat intake in the diet it is important to keep recipes containing almonds to a minimum. Use those recipes for special occasions. Almonds are best bought in their shells and shelled as required. Unshelled nuts are protected from heat, air, light and moisture and will keep almost indefinitely.

Shredded coconut: Coconuts are an excellent source of phosphorous and potassium but are high in fat. A small amount is occasionally called for to flavour a recipe but use sparingly.

Pine nuts, sunflower seeds, poppy seeds, pumpkin kernels and sesame seeds: These are used very sparingly to flavour some recipes. All can be bought at health food shops.

Vanilla essence: The pure vanilla essence is obtained by steeping the vanilla pods in alcohol (usually brandy) and water over a period of time.

Tinned and packaged foods: Use only tinned and packaged foods when fresh food is not available or is too expensive. Become a label reader! Look for natural food, without sugar, salt or other additives. It is one thing to save a few cents on an item with all the additives, but it is later in life that the cost becomes a burden.

Ginger: Peel the root before chopping up very finely. To make fresh ginger juice, place small pieces in a garlic crusher and squeeze. It is used to flavour many dishes, spicy and sweet. It is also reputed to be an excellent remedy for sore throats and stomach upsets.

Garlic: This is a bulbous plant of the onion family. The bulb is composed of many small cloves enclosed in a papery skin. It has a long history of uses, both culinary and medicinal and is said to be one of nature's most natural antibiotics. It has a very pungent flavour and enhances many dishes.

Soy sauce: A dark, almost black, thin sauce made from fermented soy beans. It enhances vegetable, meat and rice dishes. Use only a low salt variety.

Herbs: These are best grown fresh in your garden but you should also explore and decide which dried varieties suit your palate. These can be used individually or combined to create wonderful flavours in sweet or spicy recipes without the need to add salt or sugar.

Tofu: This is soy bean curd. It is made by adding a natural coagulant (lemon juice) to soy milk. Curds are created, the excess milk drained off and it is pressed into blocks form to remove all liquid. It has an excellent protein and calcium content, is low in fat and is cholesterol free. Tofu has a bland taste and can be used for salads, sweet or savoury dishes.

Brown rice: Brown rice is the natural, unpolished rice that has been hulled but still has its bran. The bran in brown rice offers additional protein, plus traces of iron, calcium and vitamin B. It has a nutty flavour and is extremely nutritious. It takes longer to cook than white rice.

Dried fruits: These include apricots, apples, raisins, sultanas, currants, bananas, peaches, nectarines and pears. Dried fruits contain a high level of natural sugar, so they should not be eaten in excess. Look for sun dried fruits without additives where possible.

Tomato paste: This is a concentrated puree of tomatoes. You can make your own tomato paste by peeling and deseeding very ripe tomatoes. Chop them up finely and cook until they thicken. Do not add any liquid.

Chicken stock: Boil up some chicken carcasses and/or meat in a combination of water and orange juice. Add onion, celery and carrot, and ginger root or garlic. Let simmer for two hours. Strain, cool and defat. Use as required.

Vegetable stock: Combine mixed vegetables and spices, cover with water and simmer for 2 hours. Strain and cool.

Sprouts: Alfalfa sprouts are the most common, but mung beans and lentils are also excellent sprouted. Buy ready sprouted or sprout your own. Alfalfa sprouts are rich in nearly all vitamins and minerals. They are a good source of protein and enzymes, as are most other sprouts.

Agar: This is a seaweed based setting agent like gelatine. It is high in protein and calcium and easy to digest. For all recipes in this book granulated agar is used. One teaspoon of agar sets approximately one cup of liquid, depending on the texture you require.

Yeast: Baker's yeast in granulated form is used in all recipes to act as a leavener for breads and pizza dough.

Natex: This is a low salt yeast extract which is similar in taste and appearance to Vegemite. It contains no artificial additives or preservatives. Use on toast or in sandwiches.

Vecon: This is a concentrated vegetable stock with vitamins. It makes a quick vegetable stock when reconstituted with water. The amount will be determined by the flavour required. Add it to casseroles, soups and gravies when a suitable stock is not available.

Peppermint essence: This is a concentrated oil from the steaming distillation of the peppermint plant.

Orange and lemon essences: These are concentrated extracts of the fruits. Use pure essences and use them sparingly.

Skim milk powder: This is milk from which the moisture has been removed. It is added to dry ingredients in baking or reconstituted by adding water.

Non fat or skim milk: This is milk with less than 1 per cent milk fat. It still contains the nutrients of whole milk except for fat soluble vitamins.

Evaporated low fat milk: This is tinned milk with a large percentage of water removed. It contains no sugar, has a heavier texture than non fat milk, and is a good substitute in recipes calling for whole milk. It is 'pure skim milk with 60 per cent of water removed and contains less than ½ per cent fat'.

Non fat buttermilk: Originally, buttermilk was the liquid drained from the churn after butter making. Today buttermilk is made by adding selected bacteria to non fat milk. It is slightly acidic in flavour, thicker in consistency than milk, and thinner than yoghurt. Nutritionally it compares with skim milk with a maximum fat content of around 0.8 per cent. Buttermilk can be substituted for milk in any recipe.

Non fat yoghurt: This is a cultured milk product. Specific bacteria are added to fresh skim milk to develop a tangy flavoured, custard-like yoghurt. It is more nutritious than milk because an extra 4 per cent of non fat milk powder is added to enhance the texture. It has a fat content of approximately 0.1 per cent.

Low fat ricotta cheese: This is made from the curd rather than the liquid milk, which is drained off. It has a bland flavour and is a mass of fine, small curd particles. It is suitable to add to savoury or sweet dishes and is delicious just as it is on vegetable crudites, wholemeal bread or wholemeal biscuits. Preferably look for cheese with 1 per cent fat content.

Non fat cottage cheese: This cheese has the consistency of paste and has a light acidic flavour though is still fairly bland. It contains a maximum of about 0.4 per cent fat. Again, it is suitable for savoury or sweet dishes.

Note: Information about these dairy foods has, in part, been obtained from the Australian Dairy Corporation.

Wholemeal flour: All recipes in this book which include wholemeal flour (or cake flour) refer to 80 per cent wholemeal flour (or cake flour). One hundred per cent wholemeal flour may be used. One hundred per cent wholemeal flour contains the highest nutrient and protein value, as well as bran for essential fibre.

Unbleached white flour: This is wholemeal flour with the bran and husks removed, but without the addition of chemicals. Use in conjunction with wholemeal flour for baking or substitute half or all with 80 per cent wholemeal flour.

Eggs: Egg whites are used in a number of recipes. Egg yolks contain fat and cholesterol and are rarely used. The egg white, when whipped to form stiff peaks, breaks down protein and these expand, forming elastic walled cells that trap air. This in turn expands when subjected to heat. This is what makes egg whites such a valuable leavening agent. Yolk protein, on the other hand, binds and thickens. It can be substituted by doubling the egg whites for the number of eggs in a recipe or by adding a small amount of another thickening and binding ingredient like arrowroot, grated or cooked apple or fresh banana. All recipes that call for eggs use 55g eggs.

Note: See egg section for comment on whole eggs and recipes.

Wholemeal bread: Choose those varieties that are salt free or low in salt, sugar free and oil free or low in oil. Those breads containing grains are an excellent choice. Introduce variations in bread types such as rye bread and sourdough. Making your own bread is one sure way of knowing what actually goes into the bread. There are wholemeal, salt free bread mixes now available in supermarkets and health food stores.

Wholemeal pita bread: Also known as flatbread or Lebanese bread, it is basically made from wholemeal flour, water and minimal salt. It is excellent just as it is, or open one end and fill with salad ingredients. It also makes an excellent pizza base.

Wholemeal filo pastry: This is excellent for wrapping food. Dry bake in the oven until filling is cooked and pastry is crisp. Because it is paper thin you will need several sheets of pastry to make a layer for the base of a pie.

Fruit juices: The best quality juices are obtained by juicing fresh fruits and vegetables and returning fruit fibre to the liquid. When buying fruit juices choose those that do not have sugar added to them and are preservative free. Do not overuse juices. Encourage children to drink plenty of water from an early age.
Herb teas: There is much nutritional value in herb teas. Children will enjoy them chilled with ice blocks and slices of lemon or lime.
Caro: This is a cereal beverage made of roasted, malted barley, barley, chicory and rye. For children who like a 'hot cuppa' with Mum and Dad, it is an excellent choice. It is caffeine free.
Carob: This is a fine dark powder. It comes from carob pods (from carob trees) which are deseeded, toasted and ground to make a sweet tasting flavouring agent. Add to cakes and treats, drinks and desserts. Use slightly more carob in recipes when substituting it for cocoa. Carob contains natural sugar. It is caffeine free, so it is preferable to chocolate or cocoa.
Apple juice concentrate: This is apple juice boiled down to a syrup. It can be reconstituted to an apple juice drink by adding water. 'Apple juice is preferred to honey because it contains vitamins, minerals and water soluble fiber (pectin) which honey does not have. Honey is approximately 80 per cent sugar and apple juice concentrate is approximately 66 per cent. Honey has 61 calories per tablespoon and apple juice concentrate has 30 calories per tablespoon.' (Nutrition Department, Pritikin Longevity Center.)

Cold compressed oil: When oil is extracted with little or no heat or use of chemical solvents, as for ordinary oils, the vitamin E content is not destroyed. Oil should be bought in brown bottles or tins, kept away from light and refrigerated. Do not use oil excessively and only in the amounts given in the recipes. I use almond oil for sweet cooking or grapeseed oil, and use recipes containing oil in moderation.

Sodium-free baking powder: All recipes in this book using flour and baking powder use commercially packaged baking powder. To maintain a diet low in sodium you can make your own sodium-free baking powder by using equal quantities of the following ingredients:

2 tablespoons corn flour
2 tablespoons cream of tartar
2 tablespoons potassium bi-carbonate (available at chemists)

Sift ingredients together and store in an air tight jar. Shake before using. Use approximately two teaspoons of this baking power for every one cup of flour. The baking powder will begin to react once it combines with moisture so you need to work quickly at this stage, placing it in the oven before it subsides.
Note: A better result in your baking of cakes may be achieved by increasing oven temperature (5 °C) and reducing cooking time (5 minutes).

herbs

	Flavour	Use
Balm: Lemon	This herb has a very strong lemon scent. The leaves are oval in shape and crinkly like spearmint.	Fresh leaves are floated on top of cool drinks. Delicious chopped into fruit salad. They give a lemon tang to a tossed green salad. Fresh or dried lemon balm may be put into a teapot with tea as a refreshing pick-me-up.
Basil	Sweet basil has light green, soft leaves. Bush basil has much smaller leaves. When broken and rubbed in the fingers, the foliage has a spicy aroma like cloves. Sweet basil has a slightly stronger perfume than bush basil.	Fresh or dry leaves go into Italian dishes, season tomatoes, eggplant, capsicum, vegetable soups, tomato sauce. The fresh leaves are excellent in a tossed salad, potato salad, rice salad, cucumber, cooked green bean salad. Basil is one of the most useful herbs.
Bay Leaves		A bay leaf is added to a bouquet garni, the other herbs being thyme, marjoram and parsley. It is used to flavour marinades, stocks, soups, poultry and fish dishes and spaghetti sauce. Bay leaves may be used fresh or dried, but should be kept in an airtight container.
Caraway	Frond-like leaves. The pungent seeds are rich in aromatic oils, and are prized for their use in cooking and as an aid to digestion. Store seeds in an airtight container.	Breads, especially rye bread. They flavour soups, stewed and baked fruits such as apples and pears. They flavour vegetables such as cabbage, carrots and cauliflower.
Chives	Onion chives have a round, hollow leaf with a mild flavour of onion. Garlic chives have a flat leaf broader than onion chives and are not such a dark green. The flavour is mildly garlic.	Chopped chives go into salads, cottage cheese and can be used as a garnish for baked potatoes, soups, entrees, fish, sauces.
Coriander	Has lacy, feathery foliage. Ripe coriander seeds are slightly oval, small and a beige colour. It has a spicy aroma.	The ground seeds are used to give a tang to fish, poultry and meat dishes. They flavour cakes, biscuits, pastries and bread. Sprinkle a little ground coriander over apples, pears and peaches while baking. A pinch flavours eggplant and capsicum.

Dill	Has delicate leaves of dark green aromatic foliage. Seeds have a pungently dry aromatic flavour (aniseed). The seeds flavour pickles, chutney, coleslaw, creamed fish, meat loaf, potato salad, cottage cheese, cabbage, cauliflower and cucumber. Dill is an excellent herb used with seafood.	The foliage, either the fresh chopped leaves or the dried crumbled leaves, flavours dips, spreads, sauces, salad dressings, coleslaw, tossed green salads, potato salad, fish and rice. Sprinkle on vegetables lightly.
Fennel	The foliage when fresh is chopped finely and sprinkled over fish while cooking, or the whole leaves are used as a stuffing for fish.	The seeds, which have digestive properties, go into pastries and breads, into fish and meat dishes and can be added to steamed cabbage while cooking. They are excellent in beetroot or potato salads.
Garlic		This pungent herb is used in a tremendous number of dishes, particularly casseroles, salads and sauces.
Marjoram	Oregano and marjoram are closely related herbs.	In pasta and rice dishes, pizza, tomatoes, eggplant, capsicum, zucchini, some meat dishes and savoury sauces.
Mint	A refreshing herb with a cool, clean flavour.	In cool drinks. Excellent with citrus fruit and pineapple, orange and onion salad, new potatoes, peas, carrots, tomato sauces, mint sauce, tomatoes.
Oregano	Has a far more pungent flavour than marjoram.	With pasta, rice, tomatoes, eggplant, capsicums, zucchini, in pizzas and savoury sauces, and also in some meat dishes.
Parsley	A long-time favourite for many reasons. It has attractive leaves useful for garnishes. It has a pleasing taste and contains many health-giving vitamins and minerals. It is also an excellent breath deodorizer after garlic and onions. It combines excellently with chopped chives.	As a garnish or chopped in soups, over salads, vegetables, pasta dishes, rice and mashed potatoes.
Rosemary	The oil in the leaves is very pungent, so use sparingly at first.	Chop leaves fresh or dice, and add them to stuffings for meat or chicken. Add to potato pastry, spinach, carrots, zucchini, eggplant.

Sage	This is one of the ingredients in mixed herbs, the others being marjoram and thyme.	In stuffing with onions. It seasons breadcrumbs for chicken or fish.
Tarragon	A strong flavoured herb, a little goes a long way. The French tarragon is recommended for culinary use. It does not set seeds. Tarragon must be dried quickly to keep its colour and flavour.	The spicy somewhat tart taste of the leaves gives a piquant flavour to poultry and fish. Add to wine vinegar, and keep aside for a dressing.
Thyme	Garden thyme is the kind most used in cooking. Thyme can be picked throughout the year to use fresh in cooking. Thyme is an ingredient in mixed herbs, together with sage and marjoram.	It seasons meat loaf, rissoles, stews, soups and strongly flavoured vegetables like onions, steamed cabbage, swede, turnips and parsnips. Thyme makes an excellent herb tea.

spices

	Flavour	Use
Allspice	A spice which has an aroma similar to a combination of cinnamon, cloves and nutmeg. The flavour is strong, so it should be used sparingly.	To flavour chutneys, relish, marinades, cakes and steamed puddings.
Cayenne	A ground spice of the chilli pepper family.	Sparingly to flavour seafood, sauces, or as an interesting addition to a basic coleslaw.
Chillies	These can come whole dried or finely ground.	To add flavour to curries or chutneys or rice dishes.
Cinnamon	This spice is the bark of a tree native to Ceylon. It is presented in a rolled-up quill form or finely ground. It would possibly be one of the most popular spices.	Adds flavour to rice dishes, curries, cooked fruits such as apples, apricots or pears, cakes and steamed puddings. Cinnamon and orange juice added to a natural yoghurt make a delicious refreshing summer dessert.
Cloves	A spice with a powerful flavour used very sparingly.	Whole cloves or ground cloves are excellent additions when cooking apples and pears, to chutneys, steamed puddings, dried fruits and some vegetable dishes.
Coriander	A spice which comes in seed or ground form. It has an orange-like flavour and adds zest to a rice dish or to curries.	
Ginger	A spicy warm flavour.	For meat and vegetable dishes it is usually teamed with other spices. For desserts, cakes and steamed puddings it should be used sparingly.
Mustard	Comes in seed or powder form. Its flavour is pleasantly poignant.	To add flavour to a white sauce, a mayonnaise or vegetable dishes.
Nutmeg	Is most suitably used fresh and grated to capture its true flavour.	A widely used spice in hot or cold drinks, spicy or sweet dishes. Try it with fish, veal, spinach, carrots, cakes and cooked fruits.
Paprika	Spice used for its flavour and colour. It is the ground seed of the sweet pepper and ranges from mild to sweet to mildly hot.	Flavours chicken, vegetables, fish and sauces. Its bright red colour sprinkled over a pale dish immediately adds warmth and interest.
Tumeric	Adds a yellow colour to most dishes.	Use to colour egg whites, rice, or use in dressings, soups and salads.

my kitchen helpers

Food processor: This will undoubtedly be your most expensive piece of kitchen equipment. It is not an essential kitchen helper, but it will greatly reduce the time taken in the kitchen for preparation of food.

Its uses include chopping, slicing, mixing and grating ingredients for soups, casseroles, lasagne, pie crusts, slices and cakes. It is also useful for mincing meat, fish and chicken, and fresh herbs.

For all recipes using a food processor in *Taste of Life, More Taste of Life* and this book, I have used a Breville Cyclonic Super Whizz. A food processor, like this one with a large motor and a large capacity bowl, is obviously preferable.

Food blender: Most things can be blended in a food processor, so this is an optional extra. However, the milk and yoghurt drinks and the whipped cream are blended more smoothly and more effectively in a blender. The rotary action of the blender is much faster than the processor.

Garlic press: This is useful for crushing garlic and fresh ginger to obtain ginger juice.

Sharp knives: Blunt knives rather than sharp ones are more likely to cause accidents in the kitchen. Use cleavers or large bladed knives for chopping. Serrated knives can be used for cutting bread, citrus fruits and slicing tomatoes or other soft foods. Use small knives for peeling and slicing small foods.

Orange rinder tool: This tool easily removes the orange zest in fine strips from the orange without the pith.

Cheese grater: A small, very fine grater is excellent for making the zest of fruit into a pulp, which adds extra flavour to food.

Non stick cookware: When not using fat or oil to cook in, it is necessary to use a non stick surface so that food does not adhere to the surface of the cookware.

***Non scratch cooking utensils:** Non stick cookware is easily scratched and the surfaces easily destroyed. Do not use metal utensils on non stick cookware; only heavy duty plastic ones or those especially designed for this type of cookware will do.

Steamer: Steaming food helps to retain the nutrient value. You can buy steaming racks to place in saucepans or a steamer saucepan set, in which one saucepan sits on top of another.

Metal spoons: When folding egg whites into other ingredients always use a metal spoon. A wooden spoon absorbs the air from the egg white.

Cutting boards: You will need one small board for garlic and onions, one for fresh herbs, one for chopping meat, and another large board for everything else. Do not wash wooden chopping boards in soapy water. Gently wipe over with warm water and lightly oil the board with a cold compressed olive oil. Wipe excess oil from the board with tissues.

Vegetable scrubbing brush: Vegetables like potatoes, carrots and parsnips only need to be scrubbed clean, not peeled. Most of the nutrient value lies below the surface of the peel; peeling, in many instances, removes the value of the vegetable.

Chinese wok: The Chinese method of cooking is the best way to present nutritious vegetables. Only a small amount of cooking time is required and vegetables retain their colour and crispness as well as their nutrient value. I use a silverstone Chinese wok with a non stick surface. To protect your wok, never use hot soapy water to clean it. After cooking, wipe out with warm water to remove small particles of cooked food. Wipe over completely with cold compressed olive oil to remove all remaining food particles. Wipe off excess oil with tissues.

Juice extractor
Set of metric measuring cups and spoons
Rolling pin
Flour sifter
Wooden spoons
Metal bowls (especially for mixing egg whites)

information about the foods in this book

The foods in this book are low in fats, low in cholesterol and low in protein — especially animal protein. They offer plenty of nutrition and much needed fibre. There is no added refined sugar or salt, and no added preservatives or artificial flavours in any of the recipes. The foods include:

- vegetables
- fruits
- legumes
- grains
- a small amount of nuts (almonds and pinenuts)
- a small amount of seeds (sesame and sunflower seeds for added flavour)
- natural sun dried fruits
- non fat and some low fat dairy products
- a small amount of lean, fat free red meat, chicken and fish.

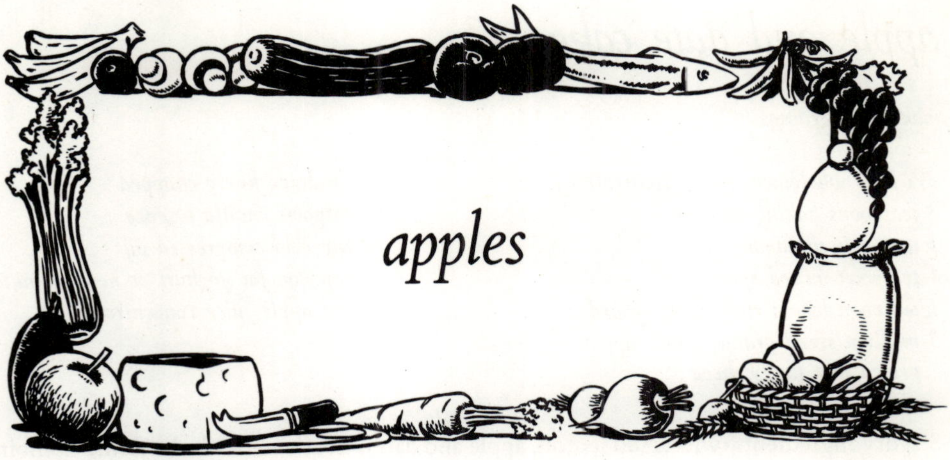

apples

apples baked with fruit filling

serves 4

4 granny smith apples
4 tablespoons dried fruit medley
½ teaspoon cinnamon
½ teaspoon mixed spice
rind of 1 orange finely grated
1 cup unsweetened orange juice

Core apples and leave whole. Peel skin from the top half. Combine dried fruit, spices and orange rind. Fill apples with this mixture. Place in a saucepan that apples will stand up in. Pour over orange juice. Cover and simmer gently until apples are just tender (approximately 10–15 minutes). Serve with low fat cream, non fat yoghurt or creamy custard.

apple snow

serves 4

4 granny smith apples
1 teaspoon lemon juice
1 teaspoon lemon zest

Place unpeeled apples in freezer for at least 8 hours. Remove and let stand for 10 minutes. Carefully remove peel and core and cut into chunks. Toss in the lemon juice and lemon rind. Place in a food processor using steel blade and process until light and fluffy.

Serve in cups with spoons or mix with kiwi fruit. Alternatively, cut a pear in half and remove core and some of the flesh. Wipe over with lemon juice and freeze for 1 hour. Scoop the apple snow onto the pear. Garnish with blueberries, kiwi fruit or fresh strawberries.

apple and date cake

makes 12 servings

2½ cups wholemeal plain flour (80%)
3 teaspoons baking powder
1 teaspoon cinnamon
1 teaspoon mixed spice
1 teaspoon lemon rind finely grated
3 medium sized granny smith apples peeled and finely diced
1 cup dates finely chopped
1 teaspoon vanilla essence
¼ cup cold compressed oil
½ cup non fat yoghurt or non fat buttermilk
½ cup apple juice concentrate

Sift dry ingredients twice. Add lemon, apple and dates. Coat well with the flour. Combine vanilla, oil, yoghurt and apple juice concentrate. Add to other ingredients and mix well. Spoon into a foil lined 20cm round cake tin. Cook at 180°C for 50–60 minutes or until firm to touch on top and an inserted skewer comes out dry. Cool in tin. Decoarte with thin slices of red and green apple.

apple salad

serves 6 approximately

2 granny smith apples
2 delicious or jonathon apples
1 small red capsicum
1 small green capsicum
2 tablespoons pine nuts roasted under griller
2 stalks celery
¼ cup clear apple juice
2 tablespoons lemon juice
1 tablespoon cider vinegar
2 tablespoons fresh mint finely chopped
2 tablespoons fresh chives finely chopped

Core apples and cut into thin wedges. Dice capsicums finely. Cut celery into thin slices. Mix apple juice, lemon juice and vinegar and combine with salad ingredients and pinenuts. Sprinkle with mint and chives. Serve with alfalfa sprouts.

apple and cheese kebabs

green and red apples
dried apricots
low fat grating cheese

Cut apples and cheese into chunks. Soak apple in iced water with lemon juice for 10 minutes if you do not intend to serve kebabs immediately. This will prevent them from turning brown. Thread the apple, cheese and dried apricots onto a wooden skewer.

apple and date bars

makes approximately 24 bars

Pastry:

2 cups wholemeal plain flour (100%)
2 cups rolled oats
½ cup cold compressed oil
¼ cup apple juice concentrate
½ cup unsweetened orange juice or
½ unsweetened orange juice and ½ lemon juice

Combine flour and oats in a food processor and process lightly. Add oil and apple juice concentrate and orange juice. Process until pastry binds together. Divide in half. Roll out pastry to make two rectangles. One should be approximately 20cmx30cm, the other slightly bigger. Place the larger piece of pastry on the base of a 20cmx30cm foil lined slice tin.

Filling:

250g dates finely chopped
2 granny smith apples peeled, cored and sliced
1 cup unsweetened orange juice
1 teaspoon orange rind finely grated

Place all ingredients in a small saucepan. Simmer for 20 minutes or until mixture is soft and most of the orange juice absorbed. Cool slightly.

Pour over base and spread evenly. Carefully cover with the top piece of pastry so that it does not break. Press down at the edges to meet the bottom layer. Cook at 180°C for 20–30 minutes. Cool in tin before cutting into bars.

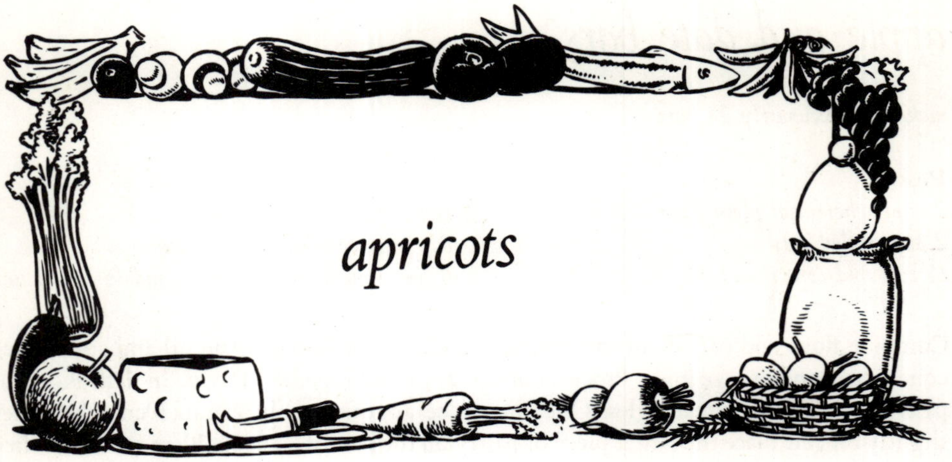

apricots

apricot thickshake

makes approximately 2 servings

cup ice cold skim milk, soy milk or goat's milk
½ cup fresh apricots finely chopped
or natural sugar free tinned apricots
2 ice blocks
1 teaspoon apple juice concentrate
¼ teaspoon cinnamon (optional)

Place all ingredients in a food blender or processor and blend until thick and creamy. Add 2 tablespoons low fat ricotta cheese for a richer, creamier thickshake.

apricot and apple oat slice

makes approximately 24 pieces

1 cup whole dried apricots
1 cup dried apples
1 cup whole almonds in their skins
1 cup shredded coconut
2 cups rolled oats
2 teaspoons orange zest finely grated
2 teaspoons lemon zest finely grated
2–4 tablespoons unsweetened orange juice

Chop apricots and dried apple finely in a food processor using the steel blade. While machine is operating, add almonds, coconut, oats, orange and lemon zests. The mixture should resemble coarse breadcrumbs. Slowly add unsweetened orange juice until mixture just starts to stick together.

Press firmly into a 20x30cm foil lined slab tin. Use a round shaped glass to roll mixture down firmly in the tin. Refrigerate. Cut into squares or shapes and keep refrigerated.

apricot crumble slice

makes 20–24 pieces

Base:

1 cup wholemeal plain flour
1 cup rolled oats
¼ cup cold compressed oil
2 tablespoons apple juice concentrate

Combine all ingredients in a food processor and process until ingredients bind together. Firmly press into a 20cmx30cm slice tin. Set aside.

Filling:

250g dried apricots
1 cup water
1 teaspoon orange rind finely grated

Place apricots, water and orange rind in a saucepan. Simmer until apricots are soft (approximately 10–15 minutes). Puree and cool slightly. Pour over base.

Crumble topping:

2 egg whites
125g almonds finely ground
1 teaspoon vanilla essence
2 tablespoons apple juice concentrate
2 tablespoons shredded coconut

Beat egg whites until stiff peaks form. Fold in all other ingredients as they are listed. Pour over apricot filling. Cook at 180°C for 20–25 minutes or until top is firm and lightly brown.

apricot, banana and apple muffins

makes 12

1 cup wholemeal plain flour
1 cup unbleached white plain flour
2 teaspoons baking powder
250g fruit freshly chopped (equal quantities of banana, apricot, apple, approximately pea size)
½ cup apple juice concentrate
2 tablespoons cold compressed oil
¼ cup non fat buttermilk
2 egg whites

Sift dry ingredients twice. Add fruit and toss in flour to coat. Combine apple juice concentrate, oil and non fat buttermilk. Add to flour and fruit and mix well. Beat egg whites until stiff peaks form and fold through the mixture. Spoon into a muffin tray. Cook at 180°C for 20–25 minutes.

overleaf: pizzas — from the top, mushroom (page 112), Hawaiian (page 113), vegetarian (page 113)

opposite: cakes — in the back row, blueberry (page 44), banana and carob filled with whipped low-fat cream and strawberries (page 35); in the front, apple and date (page 28), banana and carob muffins filled with low-fat cream and sliced bananas (page 33)

apricot and fresh fruit dip

1 cup low fat ricotta cheese
½ teaspoon vanilla essence
1 teaspoon apple juice concentrate
2 tablespoons fresh apricots finely chopped
2 tablespoons fresh strawberries finely chopped
2 tablespoons fresh pineapple finely chopped

Combine the first three ingredients and whip in a food blender or processor. Fold the fruits through carefully.

Serve on celery sticks, with chopped banana, on wholemeal bread triangles or salt free, oil free Ryevita biscuits.

apricot spread

250g dried apricots
1 cup water or unsweetened orange juice
2 teaspoons orange rind finely grated
1 tablespoon apple juice concentrate (optional)

Place all ingredients in a small saucepan and simmer until apricots are soft (approximately 20 minutes). Puree and store in sterilized jars in the refrigerator.

Serve on toast, pikelets, muffins or pancakes. Add to non fat milk for an apricot flavoured milkshake. Swirl through non fat yoghurt and chill and serve topped with fresh apricots and passionfruit pulp.

apricot loaf

makes 10–12 slices

1 cup bran
1 cup dried apricots chopped
¾ cup mixed peel or dried nectarines or peaches finely chopped
2 cups skim milk
1½ cups wholemeal plain flour (80%)
½ cup unbleached white flour
2 teaspoons baking powder

Mix bran, apricots, mixed peel and milk together in a bowl. Cover and let stand for at least 2 hours.

Sift the flours and baking powder. Add small amounts of flour to the apricot mixture and mix well. Pour mixture into a 22x12cm lined, non stick loaf tin and bake at 180°C for 45–60 minutes or until firm to touch or tap and an inserted skewer comes out dry.

bananas

banana carob muffins

makes 12

1¾ cups wholemeal plain flour (80%)
3 tablespoons carob powder
3 teaspoons baking powder
1 teaspoon cinnamon
1 teaspoon mixed spice
1 cup mashed banana
½ cup apple juice concentrate
¼ cup cold compressed oil
¼ cup non fat yoghurt
2 teaspoons vanilla essence
3 egg whites

Topping:
2 heaped tablespoons rolled oats
½ teaspoon cinnamon
1 tablespoon apple juice concentrate

Sift dry ingredients twice. Combine banana, apple juice concentrate, oil, yoghurt and vanilla. Add to flour and beat well. Beat egg whites until stiff peaks form. Fold in egg whites. Spoon into a lightly greased and floured muffin tray. Add cinnamon to rolled oats. Sprinkle over top of each muffin. Add just a drop of the apple juice concentrate. Cook at 180°C for 20–25 minutes.

banana and date wholemeal scones

makes approximately 20

2 cups wholemeal plain flour (80%)
3 teaspoons baking powder
¼ teaspoon cinnamon
¼ teaspoon mixed spice
1 cup dates very finely chopped
1 teaspoon lemon rind finely grated
1 small banana mashed
¾ cup skim milk
1 teaspoon lemon juice

Sift dry ingredients twice. Add dates and lemon rind and mix through. Combine banana, milk and lemon juice. Add this to the flour and date mixture. Mix together and knead lightly. Cut into desired shapes. Place on a non stick baking tray and cook at 230–250°C for 15–20 minutes. Eat while still warm or freeze.

baked bananas

This is an easy and delicious dessert or treat.

Wrap unpeeled bananas in foil. Cook in a moderate oven, on a barbeque or in coals for 10–20 minutes or until skins turn black and centre of bananas are soft.

Serve with skin split and a spoon to scoop out the delicate sweet fruit, top with frozen yoghurt, home made ice cream, or chopped up dried fruits.

banana and cinnamon muffins

makes 12

1 cup wholemeal plain flour
1 cup unbleached white flour
2 teaspoons baking powder
1 teaspoon cinnamon
½ teaspoon nutmeg
200g banana freshly chopped (approximately pea size)
½ cup apple juice concentrate
2 teaspoons vanilla essence
¼ cup cold compressed oil
¼ cup non fat buttermilk
2 egg whites
2 tablespoons rolled oats
extra cinnamon

Sift dry ingredients twice. Add bananas and toss in flour to coat well. Combine apple juice concentrate, vanilla, oil and buttermilk. Add to flour mixture and mix well. Beat egg whites until tiff peaks form. Fold through. Spoon into muffin tray. Sprinkle with rolled oats and extra cinnamon. Cook at 180°C for 20–25 minutes.

banana pops (bananas frozen on a stick)

Place whole, unpeeled bananas in the freezer overnight. Remove from freezer and carefully peel. Cut in half and insert a wooden stick or a corn on the cob holder.

For a special treat, dip bananas in apple juice concentrate or non fat yoghurt and then roll in finely chopped dried apricots, sunflower seeds and toasted sesame seeds or unsweetened, salt free toasted muesli.

These bananas will keep in the freezer for at least two weeks. The skin will turn black, but don't worry.

banana milkshake

serves 1

1 small ripe banana (can be frozen)
1 cup skim milk
½ teaspoon vanilla essence
dash of nutmeg (optional)
4 ice blocks

Chop banana roughly. Place all ingredients into a food blender or processor. Blend until smooth and frothy. The milkshake will be frothier and creamy smooth if you use frozen bananas.

Make this milkshake into a *banana creamy* by substituting 1 cup of non fat yoghurt for the skim milk.

bananas on porridge with yoghurt

serves 1

¼ cup rolled oats
½–¾ cup water
½ teaspoon vanilla essence (optional)
1 tablespoon sultanas

Combine all ingredients in a small saucepan and slowly bring to the boil. Simmer gently with lid on for 5–10 minutes, stirring occasionally. Pour into a serving bowl. Make a circle on top of the porridge with thin slices of banana. Fill centre of the circle with ¼ cup non fat yoghurt. Sprinkle over with nutmeg, cinnamon or finely chopped fresh strawberries.

You may like to prepare your porridge the night before. Soaking the oats brings out their natural sweetness. Cook as above. You could also substitute some of the water for natural unsweetened fruit juices or skim milk and omit the vanilla essence.

banana ice cream

1 banana = 1 serve

Place whole unpeeled bananas in the freezer overnight. Remove from freezer and carefully remove the peel. Cut banana into 4 pieces. Place into a food processor and, using the steel blade, process until thick and creamy. Eat immediately, scooped onto your favourite fruit.

Variation:
For every banana used add ¼ cup yoghurt, 1 teaspoon lemon juice and ½ teaspoon vanilla. Process as above. Pour mixture into a well chilled metal bowl and freeze for 1–2 hours. Scoop into sugar free ice cream cones.

banana and carob cake

Use the same ingredients as you did for banana carob muffins on page 33 and add an extra egg white. Spoon into a 20cm round foil lined cake tin. Cook at 180°C for 45–50 minutes. Remove from oven and cover lightly to cool. When cool, slice in half and fill with low fat cream and fresh strawberries or with custard.

To fill with custard, line the tin with foil. Place bottom half of cake back in the tin and firm cake down. Pour over cool custard. Place top on and press down lightly. Refrigerate.

Variation:
Use 1 cup of grated apple instead of 1 cup of banana.

banana custard

serves 6–8

4 cups skim milk
1 cup cornflour
2 teaspoons vanilla essence
1 tablespoon orange zest
¼ cup–½ cup apple juice concentrate
1 cup non fat yoghurt
3–4 bananas
1 tablespoon lemon juice

Bring 3 cups of milk to just below boiling. Combine 1 cup of milk, cornflour, vanilla and orange zest and mix to make a paste. Add to milk and stir briskly until thick. Cook for 2 minutes, stirring continuously. Remove from heat. Add apple juice concentrate and mix well. Add yoghurt and mix well.

Cut bananas into thin rounds and brush with lemon juice. Line a shallow baking dish with foil or plastic wrap (for easy removal). Overlap banana pieces on base of dish. Pour over custard. Refrigerate to set for at least 3 hours. Turn out and cut into squares. Top with low fat cream.

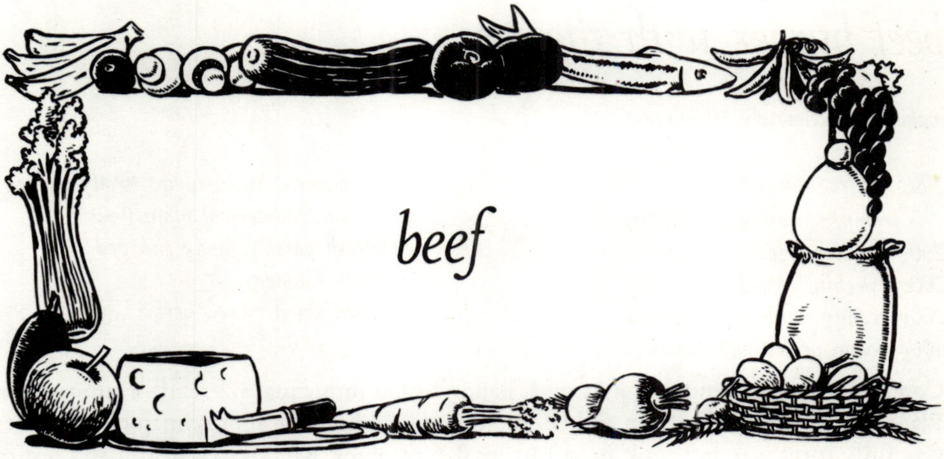

beef

beef and capsicum

serves 6

500g beef with visible fat removed
(an eye fillet would be an excellent choice)
1 large onion cut into 8 pieces
1 green capsicum cut into chunks
1 red capsicum cut into chunks
2 stalks celery sliced diagonally

Sauce:
1 teaspoon fresh ginger finely chopped
1 tablespoon salt free tomato paste
1 tablespoon low salt soy sauce
½ teaspoon dried basil
½ teaspoon dried oregano
2 cups beef stock or water
2 tablespoons cornflour

Slice meat into very thin strips. Stir fry meat (in 3 lots) to seal meat and lightly brown. Remove meat from pan. Add onion, capsicum and celery and toss, cooking for 2 minutes. Return meat to pan. Serve with hot mashed potato or brown rice.

Pour over combined sauce ingredients. Bring to the boil and then reduce heat. Simmer with lid on for 20–30 minutes. Stir occasionally so meat does not stick to base of pan.

beef and beans

serves 6

400g fat free minced beef (rump, porterhouse or fillet)
1 large onion
2 cloves garlic
1 cup salt free tomatoes and juice pureed
½ cup water
2 tablespoons low salt soy sauce
1 tablespoon toasted sesame seeds
2 stalks celery finely chopped
2 small green capsicums
400g green beans

Cook meat, onion and garlic in a small amount of water, stirring to break up meat, for 10–15 minutes. Keep covered. Add remaining ingredients and simmer, with lid off, for 15 minutes. Serve on wholemeal toast, brown rice or wholemeal pasta or cooked beans and lentils.

beef burger with the lot

makes approximately 10 burgers

500g fat free minced beef
(rump, porterhouse or fillet)
200g carrot grated
200g zucchini grated
200g granny smith apples grated
400g potato peeled and grated
1 cup wholemeal breadcrumbs firmly packed
2 tablespoons wholemeal plain flour
¼ cup fresh parsley finely chopped
½ teaspoon nutmeg
½ teaspoon dried mixed herbs

Combine all ingredients and mix with hands. Shape into equal size balls. Flatten down. Place in a lightly greased pan and cook on moderate heat for approximately 6 minutes. Carefully turn over and cook for a further 4–5 minutes. Remove from pan and rest on absorbent paper for a few minutes. Divide a wholemeal burger bun or use 2 wholemeal pita breads. Add shredded lettuce, onion rings, tomato slices, grated carrot, red and green capsicum rings, bean sprouts. Top with some homemade tomato chutney.

beef and vegetable family pie

makes 8 slices

1 quantity wholemeal bread pastry
400g fat free minced beef
1 clove garlic crushed
1 medium sized onion finely chopped
1 tablespoon water
2 cups carrots grated
1 large potato peeled and finely diced
½ cup cooked peas
2 tablespoons salt free tomato paste
½ teaspoon dried basil
½ teaspoon dried oregano
1½ cups water
1 tablespoon parsley finely chopped
2 tablespoons cornflour
2 tablespoons water

Cook onion and garlic in water until soft. Add meat, break up and simmer until meat changes colour. Add 1½ cups water and stir thoroughly. Simmer for 10–15 minutes. Add carrots, potatoes, peas, tomato paste, basil and oregano. Simmer for a further 5 minutes. Blend cornflour with 2 tablespoons of water and add to pan. Stir until thickened and allow to cool. Add parsley and stir through.

Roll pastry out to 2 thin rounds to fit a large, lightly greased pie dish. Line the dish with a round of pastry. Fill with meat mixture and top with pastry. Cook at 210–220°C for 10 minutes. Turn oven down to 180–190°C and cook for a further 15–25 minutes or until pastry gives a hollow sound when tapped. Serve hot or cold.

fruity beef luncheon loaf

serves 10–12

150g minced beef with visible fat removed
1 medium sized onion finely diced
400g potato grated
400g carrots grated
125g dried apricots finely chopped
125g sultanas
125g raisins
2 cups wholemeal breadcrumbs
⅓ cup salt free tomato paste or mango chutney (see Chicken burgers *page 60)*
1 tablespoon low salt soy sauce
½–1 teaspoon cumin
½ teaspoon coriander powder
½ teaspoon mixed spice
5 cups wholemeal breadcrumbs (for topping)

Line a dish measuring approximately 40x30x6cm with lightly greased foil. Press 2 cups breadcrumbs firmly onto base of dish. Combine all ingredients and mix well with hands. Press into dish on top of breadcrumb base and firm down. Top with breadcrumbs and firm down again. Cook at 220°C for 20 minutes. Turn heat down to 190°C and cook for further 50–55 minutes. Remove from oven. If serving hot, let stand for 10 minutes before slicing.

This loaf is excellent served hot or cold with a salad.

beef and carrot hotpot

serves 5

500g beef with visible fat removed
500g carrots cut into chunks
2 cloves garlic
1 large onion
1 cup dry red wine
½–1 teaspoon nutmeg
2 cups beef stock or water
2 tablespoons salt free tomato paste
3 bay leaves
2 tablespoons fresh parsley finely chopped

Cut meat into small pieces and then stir fry (in 2 lots) to seal and lightly brown. Remove from pan. Stir fry onions and garlic until onions are transparent (approximately 2–3 minutes). Return meat to pan. Add red wine and nutmeg and cook for 5 minutes. Add tomato paste and stock. Pour into a casserole dish. Add carrots and bay leaves. Toss well and cook at 190°C for 1¾ hours or until meat is tender. Add parsley before serving. Serve with hot mashed potato, brown rice or wholemeal noodles.

beef 'stroganoff'

serves 6

500g rump steak with visible fat removed
2 medium sized onions
250g carrots cut into thin rounds and then quartered
600g mushrooms thinly sliced
1 tablespoon Vecon
1 cup boiling water
1 cup dry red wine
2 tablespoons salt free tomato paste
ground black pepper
1 cup soy milk
1 tablespoon and 1 teaspoon cornflour

Cut steak into bite size pieces. Stir fry to seal meat and lightly brown. Remove meat from the pan. Stir fry onions until transparent (approximately 2–3 minutes). Add carrots and mushrooms and toss to combine. Dissolve Vecon in boiling water and add to pan. Simmer for 3 minutes. Return meat to pan. Add red wine and tomato paste and season to taste with black pepper. Cook 1¼ hours at 200°C in a covered casserole dish. Combine soy milk and cornflour. Remove casserole from heat and allow to cool slightly. Stir through the soy milk and cornflour until sauce becomes thick and creamy. Serve with mashed or baked potatoes.

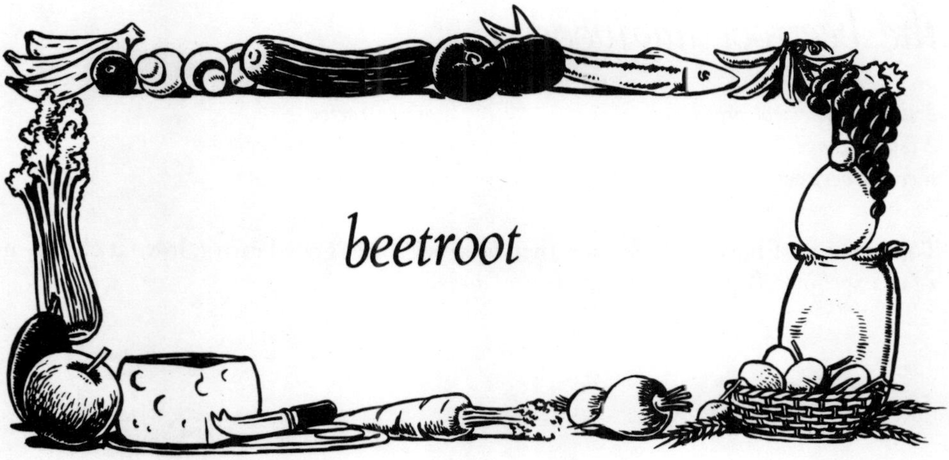

beetroot

The smaller the beetroot, the sweeter its flavour. The skins should be washed thoroughly before cooking. Simmer in enough water to cover until the beetroot is tender when tested with a skewer. To remove the skin, run under cold water and slice.

beetroot cups

serves approximately 10 depending on size of tomatoes

500g beetroot

Wash beetroot thoroughly, removing all dirt and grit. Place in a large saucepan and cover with plenty of water. Bring to the boil, turn heat down and simmer, covered, until beetroot is tender when pierced with a fine skewer. Drain and reserve liquid. While beetroot cools slightly, pour liquid through a fine sieve or piece of muslin cloth to remove any residue. Rub the beetroot skins with your hands to remove outer skins. Discard. Dice the beetroot into small squares.

Cups:
10 medium sized tomatoes
10 spring onion curls (see below)
½ cup white wine vinegar
2 tablespoons fresh basil finely chopped
black pepper to taste
2 teaspoons salt free tomato paste
1 tablespoon gelatine
1½ cups reserved cooking liquid

Remove tops from tomatoes and scoop out the seeds and flesh. Fill tomatoes with diced beetroot and top with a spring onion curl. Refrigerate until required.

Place reserved cooking liquid and gelatine in a small saucepan and slowly simmer until gelatine has dissolved. Remove from heat. Add all other ingredients, stirring thoroughly to combine tomato paste. Allow to cool slightly and pour into tomato shells over the diced beetroot, just to the top of tomato. Refrigerate to set.

Spring onion curls:
Peel outer layer from spring onion. Use a pair of scissors to snip down the green part of the onion. Make approximately 6 long cuts. Soak onions in iced water for about 1 hour so that the green part curls up.

the beetroot dagwood

2 slices wholemeal bread
2 lettuce leaves
slices of beetroot
grated carrot
grated low fat cheese
alfalfa sprouts

Top one side of bread with lettuce, then beetroot slices, grated carrot, low fat cheese, and alfalfa sprouts. Top with second slice of bread.

berries

blueberry muffins

makes approximately 12 large muffins

These are deliciously moist muffins that are best eaten warm, without adding any spreads.

2 cups wholemeal plain flour
2 teaspoons baking powder
200g fresh blueberries
¼ cup cold compressed almond oil or grapeseed oil
½ cup apple juice concentrate
¼ cup non fat yoghurt
2 teaspoons vanilla essence
2 egg whites

Sift flour and baking powder twice. Add blueberries and coat well with flour. Mix together oil, apple juice concentrate, yoghurt and vanilla. Make a well in the centre of the flour and pour in half the mixture. Gently combine without squashing blueberries. Add remaining mixture.

Beat egg whites until stiff. Gently fold egg whites through the blueberry mixture until just combined. Spoon mixture into a lightly oiled muffin tray. Cook at 180°C for 25–30 minutes. Remove from oven and eat while still warm.

berry combination thickshake

serves 2

1 cup well chilled non fat milk
¼ cup well chilled non fat yoghurt
1 cup mixed berries (blueberries, strawberries raspberries, logan berries, blackberries, etc.)
1 teaspoon apple juice concentrate

Combine all ingredients in a food blender or processor and blend until thick and frothy.

blueberry yoghurt swirl

serves 1–2

1 cup non fat yoghurt
½ cup blueberry sauce (see below)

Place blueberry sauce in the bottom of a tall glass. Add yoghurt. Using a long handled spoon, swirl blueberry sauce through yoghurt. Top with fresh blueberries and serve chilled.

Blueberry sauce:
1¾ cups unsweetened natural pear juice
⅓ cup apple juice concentrate
1 tablespoon lemon juice
2 teaspoons agar
450g fresh blueberries

Combine pear juice, lemon juice, apple juice concentrate and agar in a small saucepan. Bring to the boil. Boil for 5 minutes stirring continuously. Add blueberries and boil for 10 minutes. Pour into sterilized jars. Keep refrigerated. Use on pancakes, in muffins and on toast.

blueberry cake

makes 12 servings

2 cups wholemeal plain flour
3 teaspoons baking powder
1 teaspoon cinnamon
200–250g blueberries
¼ cup cold compressed oil
½ cup apple juice concentrate
¼ cup non fat buttermilk
2 teaspoons vanilla essence
2 egg whites

Sift dry ingredients twice. Add blueberries and toss in flour to coat well. Combine oil, and liquid ingredients. Add to flour mixture and mix well. Beat egg whites until stiff peaks form and fold through the mixture. Cook at 190°C for 35–40 minutes in a 20cm round foil lined tin.

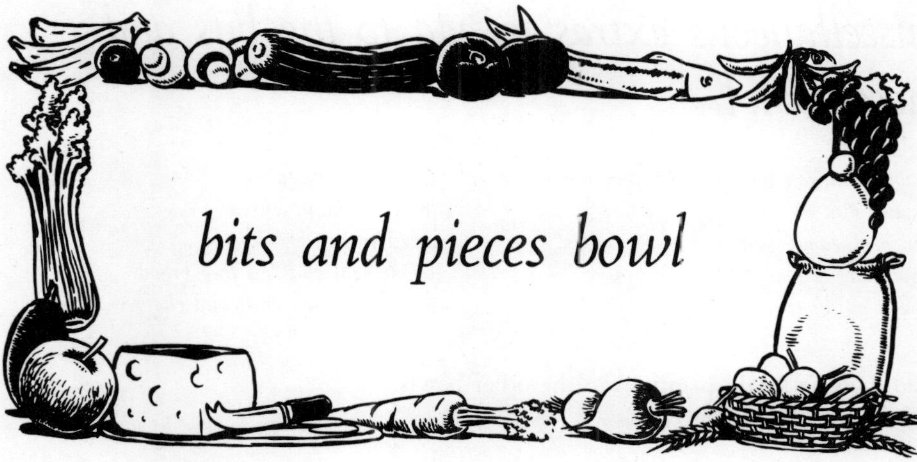

bits and pieces bowl

cooked vegetable bowl

carrot chips
pumpkin chips
potato chips
zucchini chips
sweet potato chips
beetroot chips
cauliflower heads
broccoli heads
beans
corn on the cob

Dry steam the vegetables, that is, keeping above water, or bake on a non stick tray in a hot oven. Vary the combinations.

cooked fruit bowl

apples
apricots
rhubarb
plums
nectarines
peaches

All fruits should be ripe but firm. Lightly steam fruits in a little water or unsweetened fruit juice until just tender.

the fruit bowl

strawberries
blueberries
pineapple
apples
pears
oranges
watermelon
other melons (cantaloupe, honeydew, cassava)
plums
peaches
kiwi fruit
grapes

Cut into bite size pieces. Vary the combinations depending on what fruits are in season.

miscellaneous extras to add to the bits and pieces bowl

steamed chicken with fat and skin removed
steamed fish
lean beef, lamb, veal
brown rice
cooked pulses (beans and lentils)
wholemeal pasta
low fat grating cheese
dried fruits
wholemeal and salt free bread
low fat cottage or ricotta cheese

Add these in small quantities to the other bowls.

raw vegetable bowl

lettuce leaves
cherry tomatoes
carrot sticks
celery sticks
alfalfa sprouts
mung bean or lentil sprouts
capsicum strips
cucumber rounds
zucchini sticks
asparagus spears
peas

Cut into bite size pieces or sticks. Make up different combinations of the vegetables and add a sprinkling of fresh herbs or a salad dressing. Only those salad dressings in *Taste of Life* and *More Taste of Life* are suitable.

opposite: top — beef burger with tomato sauce (page 38); chicken burger with mango chutney (page 60)

centre spread: from the back — cabbage rolls (page 52); chilli con carne beans (vegetarian) filled baked potatoes (page 71); zucchini stuffed with chilli beans (page 72)

overleaf : strawberry custard tarts (page 132) strawberry and passionfruit topped pavlova (page 131)

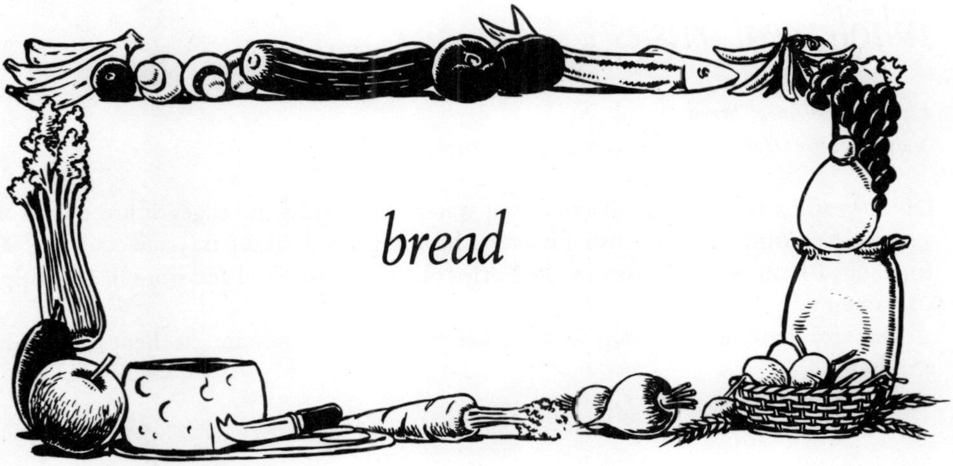

bread

For best results with bread making I use a large mixer with a bread dough attachment for kneading. You may have to knead the bread slightly longer if kneading by hand.

If using a kilogram bread pack, you may notice it does not measure exactly 2x500g flour. Top up with wholemeal flour or unbleached white bread flour.

Bread will rise faster if left in a very warm position, so it may not be necessary to leave the second time for a full 45 minutes. Wait for it to double in size before cooking.

Bread is cooked if it sounds hollow when tapped.

spicy fruit buns

makes 10

500g bread mix, wholemeal and salt free
2½ teaspoons yeast
1 teaspoon mixed spice
320ml warm water
¼ cup currants
¼ cup sultanas
¼ cup dates finely chopped
¼ cup dried apricots finely chopped
rind of one lemon
rind of one orange
½ teaspoon mixed spice
½ teaspoon cinnamon
½ teaspoon nutmeg
2 tablespoons water

Glaze:
1 tablespoon apple juice concentrate
2 tablespoons skim milk
1 teaspoon vanilla essence

Add water to flour, yeast and mixed spice. Knead for 5–7 minutes. Place in a bowl and cover with plastic wrap. Leave in a warm place to rise for 20 minutes. Roll out a rectangle approximately 25cmx35cm on a lightly floured bench.

Combine all fruits and spices. Spread evenly over the dough and press down. Use a pastry brush to wipe edges with water. Roll up like a Swiss roll and cut into 10 rounds. Place side by side on a non stick baking tray. Cover with plastic wrap and leave in a warm place for 45 minutes.

Combine glaze ingredients. Lightly wipe over tops using a pastry brush. Cook at 220°C for 10 minutes. Turn heat down to 190°C and cook for a further 5–7 minutes.

wholemeal rusks

day old wholemeal bread
Natex yeast extract (available at health food stores)

Dilute yeast extract with small amount of water. Brush sides and edges of bread with the yeast extract using a pastry brush. Place on a lightly greased baking tray and cook at 150°C for about 1 hour or until rusks are well dried out and crisp. Cool and store in an air-tight container.

Serve for dunking with soup or just as a savoury nibble. They are excellent for teething children.

wholemeal bread pastry

500g bread mix, wholemeal and salt free
2½ teaspoons yeast
320ml warm water

Combine flour, yeast and water. Mix to a firm dough. Knead for 5–7 minutes. Cover with plastic wrap and place in a warm position for 15 minutes.

Divide dough into 2 sections. Lightly flour the bench top and rolling pin and roll out the dough very thinly. Lightly grease a pie dish with cold compressed oil using a tissue to wipe out and remove excess oil. Line pie dish with bread pastry. Fill with a suitable filling such as *beef and vegetable family pie* (page 38). Roll out remaining pastry and cover pie. Seal edges using fingertips. Cut plenty of small ventilation slits around the top outer edge of the pie. Cook at 220°C for 10 minutes and turn down heat for remainder of cooking time.

wholemeal garlic bread knots

makes 10

500g bread mix, wholemeal and salt free
3 teaspoons yeast
320ml warm water
1–4 cloves garlic crushed

Make up as for *wholemeal bread pastry* adding the garlic with the water. Leave to rise for 10 minutes. Divide dough into 10 equal portions. Using your hands, roll out a long thin sausage, approximately 10–12cm long. Tie into a knot. Place the knots close together on a non stick baking tray. Cover with plastic wrap and leave in a warm position for 45 minutes. Cook at 230°C for 10–15 minutes or until browned and crisp to touch.

Variations:

Lightly brush the knots with water before baking and sprinkle with some low fat grating cheese, poppy seeds or sunflower seeds.

savoury wholemeal buns

Savoury topping:

¼ cup green capsicum finely chopped
¼ cup onion finely chopped
2 cloves garlic crushed
2 tablespoons water
¼ cup salt free tomato puree
2 tablespoons salt free tomato paste
1 tablespoon low salt soy sauce
90g grated low fat grating cheese

Wholemeal buns:

500g break mix, wholemeal and salt free
2½ teaspoons yeast
1 teaspoon dried oregano
320 ml warm water

Cook capsicum, onion and garlic in water for a few minutes to soften. Add tomato puree, tomato paste and soy sauce. Cook for 10 minutes, stirring frequently. Remove from heat and cool.

Prepare the bread as for *wholemeal bread pastry*. Knead for 5–7 minutes. Cover with plastic wrap and stand for 15 minutes in a warm position. Roll out into a large rectangle and roll up loosely like a Swiss roll. Using a sharp knife cut into 1½cm rounds. Lie flat and close together on a non stick baking tray and cover with plastic wrap. Place in a warm position for 45 minutes or until doubled in size. Before baking, spoon a heaped dessertspoon of savoury topping on top of each bun. Sprinkle with cheese. Cook at 220–230°C for 15–20 minutes.

To serve, cool slightly. Cut in half and fill with sliced tomato and cucumber or grated carrot and sprouts.

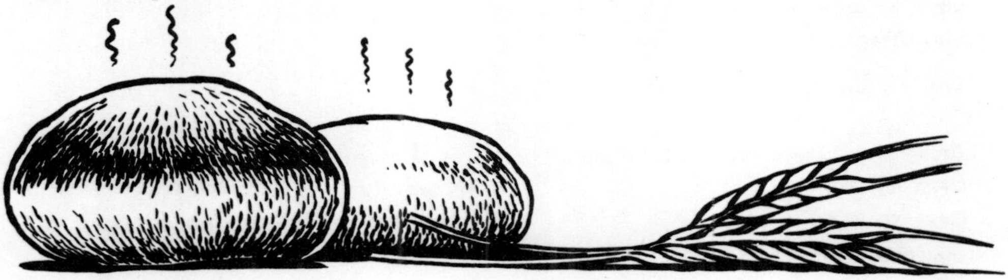

wholemeal damper

2 cups wholemeal plain flour
2 cups unbleached white flour
4 teaspoons baking powder
¼ cup non fat buttermilk
2 tablespoons lemon juice
1¼–1½ cups skim milk

Sift dry ingredients twice. Add buttermilk and lemon juice to flour. Using a knife, mix ingredients until the mixture resembles fine breadcrumbs. Add milk to make a dough which is not too sticky. Continue mixing with the knife until dough comes together.

Knead gently on a lightly floured bench. Place in a rounded flat shape on a lightly floured non stick baking tray. Make a deep incision across the top of bread to make a cross. Cook at 230°C for 15 minutes or until cooked. Damper is cooked if it sounds hollow when it is tapped from all sides.

cheesy bread sticks

makes 12

500g bread mix, wholemeal and salt free
2½ teaspoons yeast
100g low fat grating cheese
300–320ml warm water
poppy seeds

Combine all ingredients except poppy seeds. Mix to a firm dough. Knead for 5–7 minutes. Cover with plastic wrap and set in a warm position for 20 minutes.

Break dough into 12 pieces. Roll out dough into long sausage shapes approximately 16cm long. Place on a non stick baking tray. Do not let the shapes touch. Cover with plastic wrap and make air-tight. Place in a warm position for 45 minutes. Brush tops lightly with water and sprinkle with poppy seeds. Cook at 240°C for 10–15 minutes until well browned. Serve hot from the oven.

currant buns

makes 10

'Five currant buns in a baker's shop,
round and fat with a cherry on the top,
a boy came in with a penny one day,
bought a currant bun and took it away,
Four currant buns ...'

(Timothy's favourite ditty, 1984)

500g bread mix, wholemeal and salt free
3 teaspoons yeast
2 teaspoons mixed spice
1 cup currants
¼ cup skim milk or soy milk
warm water
10 glace cherries washed to remove excess sugar

Glaze:
2 tablespoons apple juice concentrate
½ teaspoon vanilla essence

Combine flour, yeast, spices and currants. Add milk to warm water to make up 300–320ml of liquid. Add to flour mixture. Mix to a firm but slightly sticky dough. Knead for 5–7 minutes. Cover with plastic wrap and place in a warm position. Leave for 15 minutes.

Divide dough into 10 equal rounds and roll lightly in wholemeal flour. Place side by side on a non stick baking tray. Cover with plastic wrap. Leave for 45 minutes or until doubled in size. Remove plastic wrap. Dip cherries in combined apple juice concentrate and vanilla. Press onto the top of each bun. Cook at 230°C for 10–15 minutes or until tops are browned and the bottom of buns crisp. While still hot, use a pastry brush to lightly wipe over the glaze.

These buns are delicious filled with mashed banana or simply eaten hot out of the oven.

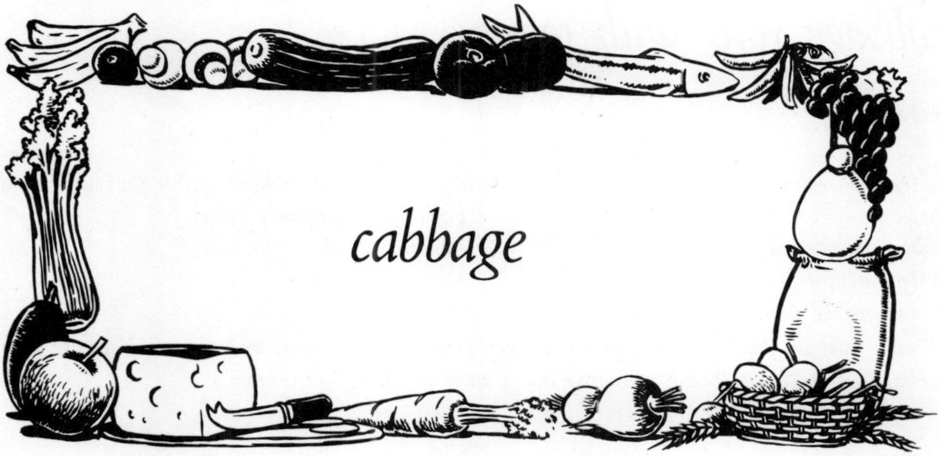

cabbage

Cabbage is high in vitamin C. A recent study shows that 'Cabbage, and members of the cabbage family (brussel sprouts, broccoli and cauliflower) may increase the output of cancer inhibiting enzymes — therefore cabbage may protect us against some forms of cancer.'

— American National Research Council of the National Academy of Sciences

vegetable coleslaw

serves 6–8

3 cups green cabbage finely shredded
3 cups red cabbage finely shredded
or
6 cups green cabbage finely shredded
½ cup carrot shredded
½ cup zucchini shredded
¼ cup celery finely sliced
¼ cup spring onions finely sliced
½ cup cooked corn kernels
¼ cup red capsicum thinly sliced
¼ cup green capsicum thinly sliced
½ cup fresh parsley finely chopped (optional)
pinch of cayenne pepper
1 cup mayonnaise (see below)

Combine all vegetable ingredients in a large salad bowl. Pour over mayonnaise and toss well. Leave to stand for at least 1 hour before serving. Served chilled.

Mayonnaise:
¾ cup chilled evaporated skim milk
¼ cup apple juice concentrate
2 teaspoons Dijon mustard
½ cup wine vinegar

Place ingredients in a screw top jar and shake well. Store in refrigerator. Shake well before using.

cabbage rolls with tomato sauce

makes 12

½ teaspoon cumin
¼ teaspoon coriander
200g carrot grated
100g zucchini grated
2 cups cooked brown rice
600g minced beef with no visible fat (rump, veal)
1 onion (approximately 100g)
½ teaspoon fresh ginger root
2 tablespoons water
18 large cabbage leaves (Choose green cabbage with thin, soft leaves and not a hard centre white cabbage, as the leaves break too easily and tend to be stringy in texture.)

Cook onion with ginger and spices in water until soft. Add meat and break up. Cover and simmer for 15–20 minutes. Continue to break meat up as it cooks, making sure all meat is well browned and cooked through. Remove from heat. Add all other ingredients and mix well. Cool.

Place cabbage leaves in boiling water and cook for 5 minutes to soften. Drain. Do 5 leaves at a time or use a large saucepan. Cut away the hard centre core, but do not cut right through the leaf. Use 1½ leaves to make a whole flat leaf. Use approximately a ½ cup of mixture to make each cabbage roll. Roll up securely, making sure the filling cannot ooze out from the sides.

Tomato sauce:
1x425g tin salt free tomatoes in juice
¼ cup salt free tomato paste
¼ cup water or dry white wine or vegetable stock
1 large clove garlic
½ teaspoon cumin
fresh parsley finely chopped to garnish

Puree all ingredients. Pour half the sauce into the bottom of a large, shallow baking dish. Place cabbage rolls, seam side down, on top of sauce and pack tightly together. Pour over remaining sauce. Cover with foil. Cook at 200°C for 30 minutes. Remove foil and cook a further 15 minutes.

Serve with a boiled or baked potato and an orange vegetable (e.g. pumpkin, carrot) or with a tossed salad. Garnish with fresh parsley.

Alternative cooking methods:
Cabbage rolls can be steamed in a steamer for approximately 30–40 minutes.
Tomato sauce can be cooked in a saucepan for 20 minutes or until thickened and poured over steamed cabbage rolls.

Variations:
Make other sauces, such as this one, to serve over steamed cabbage rolls.

White cheese sauce:
250ml soy milk
4 tablespoons cornflour
½ cup low fat grating cheese
ground black pepper to taste or a pinch of cayenne pepper

Bring all but ¼ cup soy milk to just below boiling. Make a paste with the remaining milk and cornflour. Stir through to thicken. Cook for 2 minutes. Add cheese and stir through to melt. Season with pepper.
Or
Sprinkle a cup of wholemeal breadcrumbs over the top of cabbage rolls after 30 minutes cooking time. Cook for a further 15
Or
Sprinkle over ½ cup low fat grating cheese 10 minutes before cabbage rolls are cooked. Cheese should be just melted, not well browned.

Hawaiian coleslaw

serves 4–6 as a main course

4 cups green cabbage finely shredded
1 cup fresh pineapple chunks or unsweetened tinned pineapple pieces
1 cup green capsicum strips
1 cup red capsicum strips
½ cup carrot diced
½ cup mayonnaise (see Vegetable coleslaw *page 51**)*
¼ cup unsweetened pineapple juice

Combine all ingredients in a salad bowl. Combine mayonnaise and pineapple juice. Pour dressing over coleslaw and toss well. Chill for at least 1 hour before serving.

fruity coleslaw

serves 6–8 as a main course

6 cups white cabbage finely shredded
2 oranges, peeled and segmented
¼ cup dried apricots cut into thin strips
¼ cup dried peaches cut into thin strips
¼ cup spring onions finely sliced
¼ cup celery finely sliced
¼ cup shredded coconut (optional)
1 cup fresh pineapple or unsweetened tinned pineapple pieces
2 teaspoons orange zest
2 teaspoons lemon zest
½–1 cup orange dressing (see below)

Combine all ingredients in a large salad bowl. Pour over orange dressing and toss well. Leave to stand for at least 1 hour before serving. Serve chilled.

Orange dressing:
1 cup unsweetened orange juice or Viten Juice
2 teaspoons arrowroot or cornflour
1–2 teaspoons white wine vinegar

Combine all ingredients in a small saucepan. Bring to the boil, stirring until sauce thickens. Cool and refrigerate.

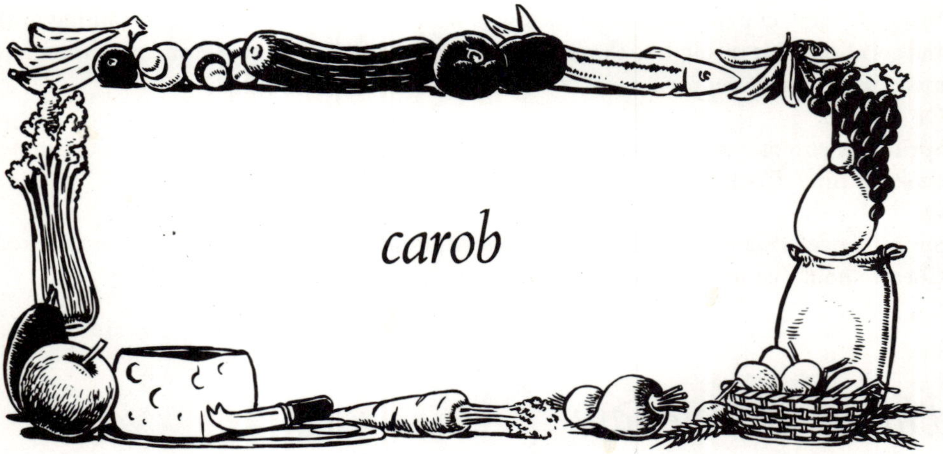

carob

carob thickshake

serves 2

1 cup well chilled skim milk
2 tablespoons skim milk powder
1 tablespoon carob powder
1 teaspoon vanilla essence
nutmeg
½ banana chopped (optional)

Place all ingredients in a food blender or processor and blend until smooth and frothy. Pour into a tall glass full of ice blocks. Garnish with a sprinkle of nutmeg.

carob peppermint hedgehog balls

1 cup dates
1 cup raisins
1 cup whole almonds in their skins
2 cups rolled oats
1 cup shredded coconut
2 tablespoons carob powder
1 tablespoon vanilla essence
½ teaspoon peppermint essence

Place dates and raisins in food processor and cut into small pieces. Add almonds, rolled oats, coconut and carob powder. Process until mixture resembles breadcrumbs. Add essences. Mixture should now begin to stick together. Stop motor and check if the texture is correct by taking a small amount in the palm of your hand and rolling up firmly into a ball. If mixture does not bind, add 1 tablespoon apple juice concentrate or unsweetened orange juice. Mixture should not be too sticky. Roll into small balls and refrigerate until firm. Keep in the freezer and use as required.

Variation:
Omit peppermint essence and press mixture into a 20x30cm slice tin. Roll down firmly using a round glass. Refrigerate and cut into slices when firm.

carob mousse

serves 6

4 cups skim milk
1 cup cornflour
2 teaspoons vanilla essence
¼ cup carob powder
4 tablespoons boiling water
1 tablespoon orange zest
½ teaspoon orange essence
1 cup non fat yoghurt
4 egg whites
strawberries

Place 3 cups of milk in a saucepan and bring to just below boiling. Add 1 cup of milk to cornflour and mix to a smooth paste. Add vanilla. Combine the carob with the boiling water and mix to a paste to dissolve the carob. Add orange zest and orange essence. Combine cornflour and carob. Add this to the heating milk and stir continuously until sauce thickens. Remove from heat and fold through yoghurt. Beat egg whites until stiff peaks form. Gently fold egg whites through the mixture. Pour into a mould or individual glasses. Refrigerate for at least 2 hours. Serve topped with fresh strawberries.

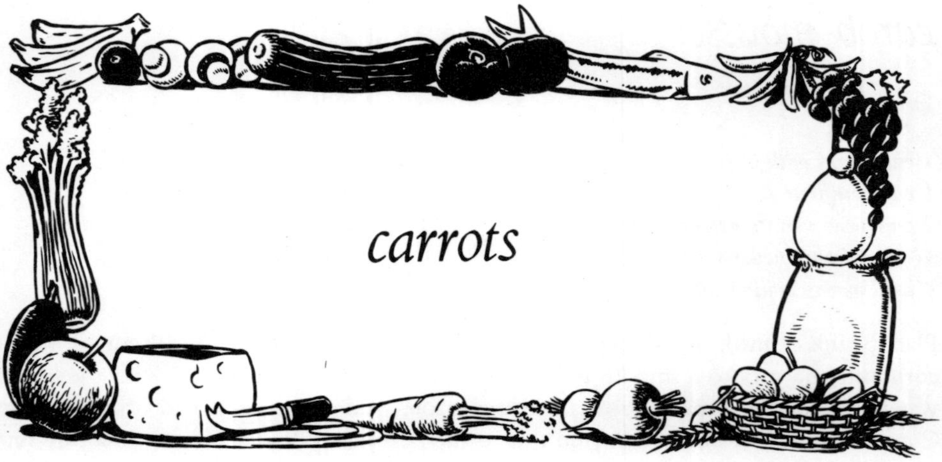

carrots

carrot and currant dip

1 cup low fat ricotta cheese
2 tablespoons non fat yoghurt
¼ teaspoon basil
¼ teaspoon oregano
1 tablespoon fresh parsley finely chopped
½ cup grated carrot
½ cup currants

Place the first five ingredients in a food processor and process until smooth. Fold through other ingredients.

Serve with chunks of wholemeal bread or carrot crackers or in pita bread pockets filled with alfalfa sprouts.

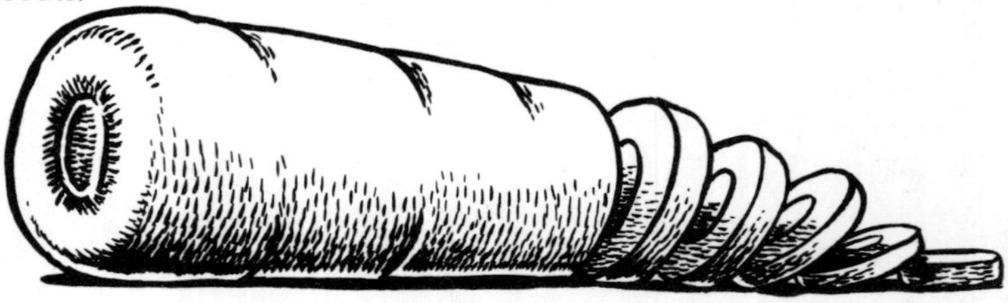

carrot and pineapple muffins

1 cup wholemeal plain flour
1 cup unbleached white flour
2½ teaspoons baking powder
1 teaspoon mixed spice or
½ teaspoon nutmeg and ½ teaspoon cinnamon
100g carrot finely grated
100g fresh pineapple finely chopped (if using tinned pineapple make sure it has no added sugar and drain it well)
½ cup raisins finely chopped
½ cup apple juice concentrate
⅓ cup non fat buttermilk
2 teaspoons vanilla essence
¼ cup cold compressed oil
2 egg whites

Sift dry ingredients twice. Add carrot, pineapple and raisins and coat well with flour. Combine apple juice concentrate, buttermilk, vanilla and oil. Add to flour mixture and mix well. Beat egg whites until stiff peaks form. Fold through the mixture. Spoon into a muffin tray. Cook at 180°C for 20–25 minutes.

carrot cake with lemon cheese topping

serves 12

2 cups carrot finely grated
1 cup sultanas
1½ teaspoons cinnamon
½ cup unsweetened orange juice
½ cup apple juice concentrate
⅓ cup cold compressed oil
1 cup wholemeal plain flour
1 cup unbleached white flour
3 teaspoons baking powder
2 egg whites

Place carrot, sultanas, cinnamon, orange juice and apple juice concentrate in a saucepan and gently bring to the boil. Simmer for approximately 5–7 minutes or until sultanas are soft. Remove from heat and leave to get cold. Add the oil and mix well. Combine the sifted flours and baking powder with the carrot mixture in 2 lots, mixing well. Beat egg whites until stiff and gently fold through the mixture. Spoon into a lined ring tin. Cook at 180°C for 45–50 minutes.

Cake should be completely cool before adding the topping.

Lemon cheese topping:
1 cup cold lemon topping (see pancake party, page 107)
100g low fat ricotta cheese

Blend ingredients until smooth and refrigerate until topping is quite firm. Spread evenly over the top of the cake.

carrot terrine

serves 10–12

500g carrots peeled and chopped
250g potato peeled and chopped
2 bay leaves
½ cup salt free and sugar free tomato juice
¼ cup vegetable or chicken stock
1 large onion finely chopped
½ cup wholemeal plain flour
½ teaspoon sage
2 teaspoons basil
1 teaspoon oregano
4 egg whites

Simmer the first six ingredients in a covered saucepan for 20 minutes or until vegetables are soft. Remove bay leaves and puree vegetables. Add flour and spices and mix well.

Beat egg whites until light and fluffy. Fold through the mixture. Pour into a lightly greased glass terrine dish (approximately 20x10cm). Cover with foil. Cook at 190°C for 40–60 minutes. Terrine is cooked when a knife inserted into the centre comes out clean. Rest for 5–10 minutes before serving. This recipe is best eaten cold so refrigerate after terrine has cooled.

Serve in sandwiches, on wholegrain rolls, salt free, oil free Ryevita or with a salad or vegetable crudites.

Variation:
Spread 1½ cups low fat ricotta cheese on top of the terrine. Decorate with sprigs of parsley or ½ rounds of cucumber with seeds removed.

cauliflower

cauliflower cheese bake

serves 4

300g carrots cut into rounds
500g cauliflower cut into flowerettes
2 cups soy milk
2 bay leaves
black pepper to taste
2 tablespoons parsley finely chopped
4 tablespoons cornflour
100g low fat grating cheese finely grated

Steam carrots and cauliflower until just tender. Combine remaining ingredients except cornflour and cheese in a small saucepan. Combine cornflour with a small amount of water to make a paste. Bring the soy milk and ingredients to just below boiling. Stir through the cornflour briskly to make a thick sauce. Remove bay leaves.

Place carrots on the base of a shallow casserole. Top with cauliflower and pour over the white sauce. Sprinkle over with cheese. Cook at 200°C for 10–15 minutes or until top is browned.

cherries

cherries in a bag

When shopping at the greengrocers, ask if a small bunch of cherries can be washed and packed in a plastic bag or punnet. Then let children carry their own bag or punnet of treats. If unable to wash fruit at the shop, do so when you get home and return them to the container for the child to eat as required. This idea works just as well with grapes.

a ribbon of cherries

Tie a coloured ribbon through the stems of cherries so that when children pull at the cherry the stem pulls away easily. Use a curling paper ribbon and then, when children finish the cherries, all the stems can be easily discarded.

chicken

chicken burgers

makes 4

200g chicken with fat and skin removed
1 granny smith apple peeled and grated
50g low fat grating cheese
1 cup wholemeal breadcrumbs
2 tablespoons fresh chives finely chopped
2 tablespoons fresh parsley finely chopped

If doubling recipe, do not double quantity of cheese. Add 25g extra cheese for 200g extra chicken.

Mince chicken. Add other ingredients and mix well. Form into 4 balls and flatten. Cook in a non stick pan for 2 minutes on both sides. Serve in a wholemeal burger bun or between 2 wholemeal pita breads. Add shredded lettuce, cucumber slices, grated carrot, alfalfa sprouts, thin slices of apple, bean shoots or sliced celery. Top with some homemade mango chutney.

Mango chutney:
flesh of 2 mangoes (approximately 420g)
2 granny smith apples peeled and grated
1 onion peeled and diced
1 teaspoon fresh ginger finely chopped
¼ cup water or chicken stock
1 cup unsweetened orange juice
⅓ cup brown rice vinegar (macrobiotic, available at health food stores)
½ teaspoon chilli powder
½ teaspoon cumin
rind of 1 orange
½ cup apple juice concentrate

Simmer onion and ginger in chicken stock for 5 minutes. Add all other ingredients. Cover and bring to the boil. Remove lid and cook for 1 hour. Stir frequently to prevent chutney sticking to the base of saucepan. Cool. Pour into sterilized jars. Keep refrigerated.

chicken and fruit curry

serves 4–6

400g chicken meat with skin and fat removed
2 cloves garlic crushed
1 large onion diced
1 tablespoon curry powder
2 cups chicken stock
2 bay leaves
1x425g tin unsweetened apricot halves drained
1x440g tin unsweetened pineapple pieces drained
6 water chestnuts thinly sliced
1 cup soy milk
1 tablespoon and 1 teaspoon cornflour

Stir fry chicken on a hot non stick surface to seal meat and lightly brown. This will take approximately 3 minutes. Remove chicken from pan. Add garlic, onion and curry powder. Toss continuously until onion is transparent (approximately 2–3 minutes).

Add chicken stock and bay leaves and bring to the boil. Add chicken meat and simmer for 20 minutes or until chicken is tender. Add apricots, pineapple and water chestnuts. Combine soy milk and cornflour to make a paste. Add, stirring continuously until sauce boils and thickens. Serve with brown rice.

chicken chausseur

serves 6–8

1kg chicken drumsticks and wings with skin and fat removed
600g carrot cut into chunks
400g mushrooms
2 cloves garlic crushed
2 tablespoons low salt soy sauce
1 cup dry white wine
1x425g tin salt free tomatoes pureed
2 tablespoons salt free tomato paste
¼ teaspoon dried tarragon
¼ cup spring onions chopped
2 tablespoons fresh parsley finely chopped

Sauce:
1 onion thinly sliced
½ cup grated parsnip
⅓ cup cornflour
3 cups chicken stock

Stir fry chicken to seal meat and slightly brown. Do in 3 lots. Remove chicken and set aside. Stir fry onion and parsnip until onion is transparent (approximately 3 minutes). Add combined cornflour and stock. Bring to the boil, reduce heat and simmer for 10 minutes. Remove sauce from pan and set aside.

Wash pan and stir fry garlic and mushrooms in soy sauce until mushrooms are soft. Add wine and boil until liquid has reduced by half. Add combined pureed tomatoes, tomato paste and tarragon. Stir to combine.

Add onion and parsnip sauce to the pan. Add chicken and carrots. Cover or place all ingredients in a covered casserole dish. Cook at 200°C for 40 minutes or until chicken and carrots are tender. If cooking on top of the stove, keep casserole simmering, stirring occasionally so ingredients do not stick to the base of pan. Serve with brown rice, mashed potato or wholemeal noodles.

chicken casserole with snow peas

serves 4

400g chicken meat with skin and fat removed
½ teaspoon cumin
½ teaspoon coriander powder
2 cups chicken stock
200g carrots
200g zucchini
100g celery
100g snow peas
5 spring onions
2 tablespoons cornflour
2 tablespoons water

Cut the chicken into bite size pieces. Heat a non stick pan to moderately hot and add chicken pieces. Keep tossing to seal the meat. This will take approximately 3 minutes. Add spices and continue to toss. Add stock and bring to the boil. Reduce heat to simmer and cook for 10–15 minutes.

Cut carrots and zucchini into rounds and then quarters. Slice the celery diagonally. Add to meat, cover and simmer for a further 10 minutes. Add combined cornflour and water. Top and tail snow peas, slice onions diagonally and add to pan. Cook 5–8 minutes, stirring continuously. Serve on a bed of wholemeal spaghetti.

chicken wings

24 chicken wings with skin removed

Marinade:
1 cup non fat yoghurt
2 tablespoons salt free tomato paste
2 tablespoons lemon juice
½ teaspoon cumin
¼ teaspoon coriander
¼ teaspoon chilli

Combine all marinade ingredients. Marinate chicken wings in marinade for at least 4 hours or preferably overnight. Remove from marinade and cover in wholemeal breadcrumbs. Shake off excess crumbs. Place in an oven bag or lie on a lightly greased sheet of foil. Cook at 200°C for 20–30 minutes or until browned evenly. Serve hot or cold with salad.

Variation:
This recipe is also suitable for fish. The quantity of marinade is enough for 8 fish fillets.

Chinese-style cooking is the easiest and the most nutritious way to present vegetables to children.

There is no need to cook the food in oil. It is just as tasty, if not tastier, cooked in stock. This is usually a combination of a good Chinese chicken stock and other flavourings like low salt soy sauce, salt free tomato paste, garlic, fresh ginger and Chinese spices.

To cook Chinese style, you will need a heavy non stick wok or large non stick pan. The wok will give best results because it spreads the heat over the base and sides, thus cooking the food evenly. The trick is to have the heat high when you start cooking, and then reduce it so that the temperature is retained without burning the vegetables. Always serve Chinese dishes immediately so vegetables retain their crispness.

chicken sweet and sour

serves 6

500g chicken with fat and skin removed
1 medium sized red capsicum
1 medium sized green capsicum
2 medium sized carrots
2 medium sized zucchinis = courgettes
6 spring onions
3 stalks celery
½ cup chopped pineapple

Sauce:
1 cup unsweetened apple juice
1 teaspoon fresh ginger finely chopped
2 teaspoons low salt soy sauce
1 tablespoon salt free tomato paste
1 clove garlic crushed (optional)

Cut chicken into 2cm chunks. Cut vegetables into even sized pieces. Combine all sauce ingredients in a wok or large shallow pan. Bring to the boil and simmer gently. Add chicken. Cook for 15–20 minutes or until tender.

Remove chicken. Turn up heat. Add all vegetables and cook for 2 minutes, tossing continuously through the sauce. Add chicken and pineapple. Place lid on wok or pan and cook a further minute. Serve on a bed of hot brown rice.

Chinese chicken stock

1 kg chicken with skin and visible fat removed
½ lemon
1 onion
1x2–3cm piece ginger root peeled
1 litre of water (add more if using larger chicken)
1 cup unsweetened orange juice

Place all ingredients in a large saucepan. Chicken should be just covered with liquid. Bring to the boil, reduce heat and simmer for 1 hour. Remove chicken and cover with cold water until completely cold. This retains moisture and makes the chicken succulent. Strain. Cool stock, refrigerate and defat. Stock is ready to use. Chicken meat can be used in the bits and pieces bowl or sliced for sandwiches.

overleaf: Drinks — back row — mineral water with ice block fruits (page 76); apricot thickshake with kiwi fruit umbrella (page 30); sparkling apple juice with fruits (page 76); middle — blueberry thickshake with blueberry stirrer (page 43); carob thickshake with lemon and banana fruit stick (page 54); front — peppermint refresher (page 77); pink fizz (page 77)

centre spread: top — Mexican lamb balls with potatoes and peas (page 95); lower left — roast lamb dinner with steamed broccoli, potato, pumpkin, cauliflower and zucchini (page 96); lower right — roast lamb dinner with steamed carrots, potato, beans and baby yellow squash (page 96)

opposite: slices: left — muesli fruit bars (page 74); apple and date bars (page 29); middle — apricot and apple oat slice (page 30); basic muesli munchies (page 75); right — apricot crumble (page 31); golly wolly banana logs (page 73)

Chinese vegetables and other favourite Chinese dishes

cabbage chop suey

serves 6–8

500g Chinese cabbage shredded
125g mushrooms chopped
125g beans chopped
4 celery sticks diagonally sliced
2 onions cut into thin wedges
1 large carrot diced
1 small red capsicum
1 small green capsicum
200g fresh bean shoots
1 teaspoon ginger root finely chopped
1 clove garlic crushed
2 tablespoons low salt soy sauce
1 tablespoon salt free tomato paste
2 tablespoons dry sherry or Chinese wine
1½ cups Chinese chicken stock
1 tablespoon cornflour.

Optional extras:
250g lightly steamed chicken cut into bite size pieces
or
250g cooked green prawns shelled and with back vein removed
or
½ cup almonds roasted under a griller until dark brown.

Place ginger, garlic, soy sauce, tomato paste, sherry, ½ cup stock and mushrooms in a cold wok. Slowly bring to the boil and simmer, covered, for 1 minute.

Remove lid and add beans, celery and onions. Toss to combine all ingredients. Cook, covered, for 2 minutes.

Remove lid and add carrot, capsicums and cabbage. Toss to combine all ingredients. You will need to do this at least twice as the cabbage softens. Cook, covered, for 3 minutes.

Remove lid and add the remaining stock combined with the cornflour. Stir through until sauce boils and begins to thicken. Add bean shoots and optional extras. Toss ingredients to combine and cook for a further 2–3 minutes. Serve immediately.

sweet and sour vegetables

serves 6–8

2 tablespoons salt free tomato paste
2 tablespoons low salt soy sauce
1 teaspoon fresh ginger root finely chopped
¾ cup unsweetened pineapple juice
¼ cup white wine vinegar
¼ cup Chinese chicken stock
1 small onion sliced into rings
1 medium sized red capsicum
1 medium sized green capsicum
200g carrots cut diagonally and in half again
200g mushrooms sliced
200g celery cut diagonally
200g zucchini cut into small chunks
1x440g tin unsweetened pineapple pieces
1 cup Chinese chicken stock
1 tablespoon and 1 teaspoon cornflour
6 spring onions diagonally sliced

Add the first 6 ingredients to a cold wok. Slowly bring to the boil and simmer covered for 1 minute. Add onions, carrot, celery and zucchini. Toss to combine all ingredients. Cook, covered, for 2 minutes.

Add capsicums and mushrooms. Toss to combine all ingredients. Cook, covered, for another 2 minutes.

Add pineapple pieces and combined remaining stock and cornflour. Wait for sauce to boil, and cook, covered, for further 3 minutes. Serve immediately, garnished with spring onions.

Chinese spring rolls

makes 10

600g shredded cabbage
1 medium sized red capsicum diced
8 spring onions finely chopped
125g mushrooms finely chopped
8 water chestnuts diced
500g cooked prawns chopped
or
500g cooked chicken chopped
1 teaspoon fresh ginger root chopped
2 tablespoons dry sherry
1 tablespoon low salt soy sauce
1 tablespoon apple juice concentrate
1 tablespoon cornflour mixed with ¼ cup water
2 teaspoons low salt soy sauce
2 tablespoons water
20 sheets of wholemeal filo pastry

Combine the first 10 ingredients and, using hands, mix well. Let stand for 30 minutes, frequently tossing flavourings through the vegetables. Place ingredients in a strainer to allow excess liquid to drain away. Use 2 sheets of filo pastry per roll. Fold in half. Turn the filo pastry sheet around so that a corner faces you. Spread ingredients across the pastry. Turn corner over filling and wipe all remaining edges with water and cornflour. Fold over edges and roll up into a long roll. Repeat with remaining ingredients.

Place on a non stick baking sheet. Wipe over tops with soy sauce and water. Do not soak the pastry. Cook at 220°C for 20 minutes. Serve immediately.

Chinese corn and vegetable combination

2 teaspoons fresh ginger root finely chopped
2 cloves garlic crushed
1 tablespoon low salt soy sauce
2 tablespoons Chinese wine or dry sherry
½ cup unsweetened orange juice
2 medium sized onions cut into quarters
3 sticks celery sliced diagonally
250g green beans sliced diagonally
250g carrots sliced diagonally
125g mushrooms sliced
125g snow peas stringed, topped and tailed
1x225g tin baby corn rinsed to remove salt
200g fresh bean shoots
1 cup Chinese chicken stock
1 tablespoon cornflour

Add the first 5 ingredients to a cold wok. Slowly bring to the boil and simmer for 2 minutes.

Add onion and celery. Toss to combine ingredients and cook, covered, for 2 minutes.

Add beans, carrot, mushrooms and snow peas. Toss and cook for 3 minutes.

Add corn and cook, covered, for 1 minute. Pour over combined stock and cornflour. Return to the boil. Add bean shoots. Cook, covered, for 1 minute. Serve immediately.

Chinese greens

serves 6

2 teaspoons fresh ginger root finely chopped
2 tablespoons Chinese wine or dry sherry
2 tablespoons apple juice concentrate
1 cup Chinese chicken stock
500g broccoli heads broken into flowerettes
1 medium sized onion cut into rings
200g green beans sliced diagonally
1 green capsicum seeded and cut into strips
4 sticks celery cut diagonally
200g snow peas stringed, topped and tailed
1 small bunch spinach with leaves only cut into strips
1 cup unsweetened orange juice
1 tablespoon and 1 teaspoon cornflour
4 spring onions diagonally sliced

Add the first 4 ingredients to a cold wok. Slowly bring to the boil and simmer, covered, for 2 minutes.

Add onion and cook for 2 minutes or until onion begins to turn transparent. Add remaining vegetables. Toss to combine all ingredients and bring back to the boil. Cover and cook for 3 minutes.

Combine orange juice and cornflour and add to the pan. Toss to combine all ingredients. Cover and cook a further 3 minutes, tossing occasionally. Garnish with sliced spring onions and serve immediately.

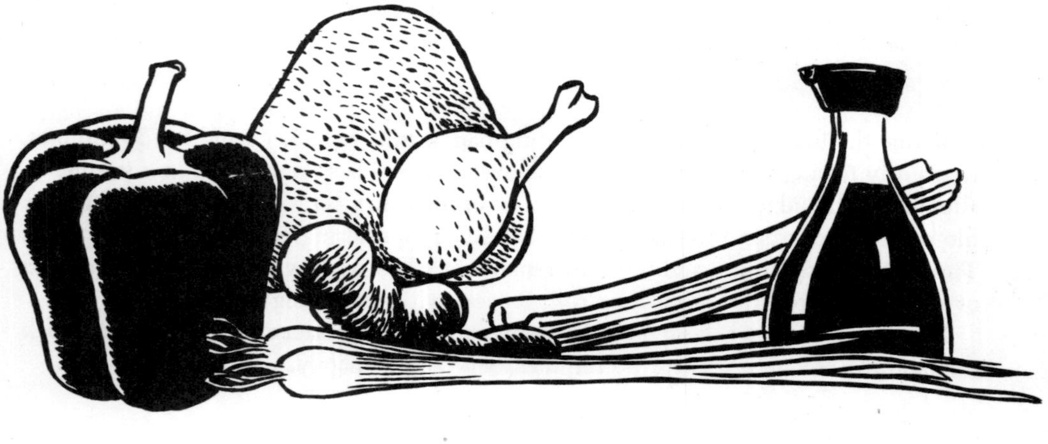

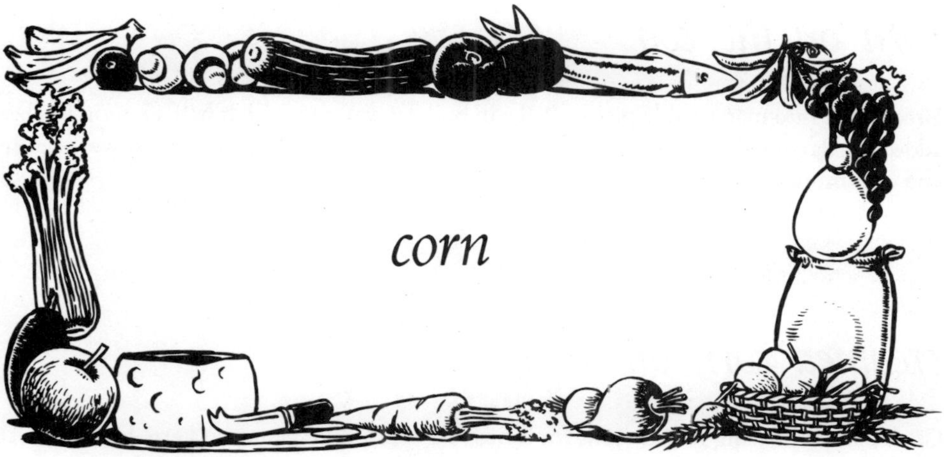

corn

Corn is an excellent source of dietary fibre and a good source of vitamin A, thiamin, phosphorus and potassium. It also contains some calcium, iron and protein.

corn chowder

Stock:

1kg chicken with skin and visible fat removed
2 corn cobs with husks removed
1 onion
1 carrot
2 sprigs parsley
1x2cm piece ginger root peeled

You will use approximately 1 cup of shredded chicken meat for this soup. The remaining chicken can be stored for other meals. The large chicken will ensure a tasty chicken stock, but you could substitute it with chicken carcasses or chicken breasts.

Place chicken stock ingredients in a large saucepan and cover with water. Bring to the boil, reduce heat and simmer gently for 1½ hours. Remove chicken and cover immediately with cold water. This will keep the chicken meat very moist. Remove from water when completely cold and refrigerate.

Soup:

1 teaspoon fresh ginger root finely chopped
1 medium sized onion peeled and diced
2 teaspoons sesame seeds toasted
6 cups chicken stock (from above)
2 egg whites
4 tablespoons cornflour
4 tablespoons water
2 tablespoons dry sherry (optional)
6 shallots finely chopped

Shred a cup of chicken and set aside. Strain the stock and discard ingredients except corn. Reserve 6 cups of stock. Use a sharp knife to cut through the corn kernels in the centre from top to bottom. Use the back edge of the knife to press the corn flesh out without pulling away the skin of the corn kernel. Set aside.

Place ginger, onion and sesame seeds in a non stick saucepan and cook gently over dry heat until onions begin to soften (approximately 2–3 minutes). If onions begin to stick, add a little stock and turn down heat. Add chicken stock, shredded chicken and corn and bring to the boil. Mix cornflour with water to make a paste. Stir through the soup until it thickens and then reduce heat. Beat egg whites lightly with 2 tablespoons water. Add this to the soup, stirring continuously. Remove from heat, add spring onions and serve.

corn on the cob

Break corn into manageable pieces. Place in boiling water to which half a lemon has been added for flavour. Cook for 3–6 minutes, depending on size. Place a corn skewer at either end and munch away.

creamed corn on toast

Cook corn following instructions for *corn on the cob*. Drain. Cut corn kernels through the centre from top to bottom of the cob using a sharp knife. Use a small spoon or blunt edge of a knife to scoop centre of corn from outer skin. Puree this mixture and spread over wholemeal toast.

You could add some grated low fat cheese and pop under the griller for a few minutes.

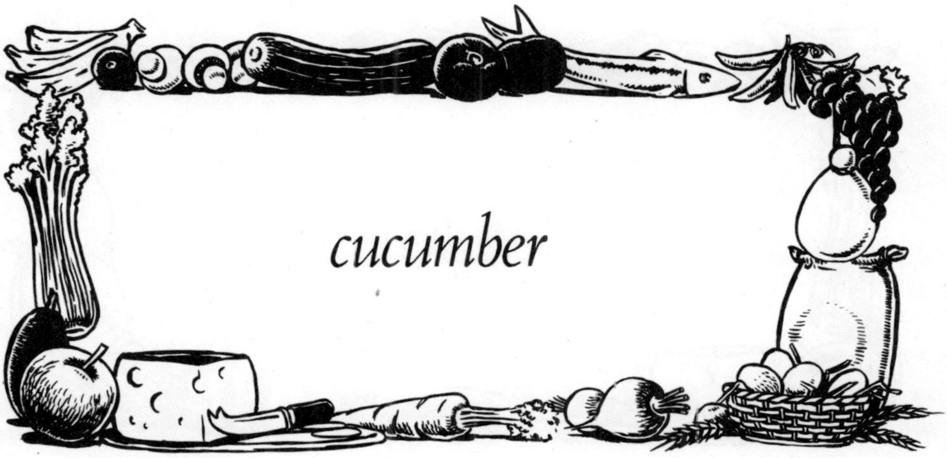

cucumber

cucumber and yoghurt dip

1 cup non fat yoghurt
¾ cup grated cucumber
2 tablespoons fresh chives or dill finely chopped

Combine all ingredients and mix well. Chill and serve with vegetable crudites or wholemeal bread chunks for dunking.

cucumber boats

serves 6

Peel a long green cucumber. Cut in half lengthwise. Remove seeds leaving a hollow down each centre. Cut a thin slice from base of each half so they sit flat, with hollow exposed. Cut 6 pieces of celery approximately 4cm high. Place a cherry tomato on top of each piece of celery, securing with a wooden toothpick.

Secure celery to cucumber with lightly beaten low fat ricotta cheese. Press celery pieces into 6 evenly placed small spoonfuls of cheese. To make oars, use long strips of carrot or long green beans and set one either side of the celery oarsmen resting in the cucumber. To make these look like boats set on blue cellophane paper (water). To serve, cut into 6 pieces so that each person receives an oarsman with oars.

cucumber pots filled with carrot sticks and celery sticks

Peel a long green cucumber. Remove ends to expose seeds. Cut into approximately 6 pieces and hollow out seeds. Cut into rounds with hollow centres. Stand cucumber rounds on top of each other to make two pots.

Remove long fibres from celery and cut into long thin pieces. Do the same with some carrots. Crisp up in ice cold water. Place in the centre of cucumber pots. Serve as nibble food with interesting dips.

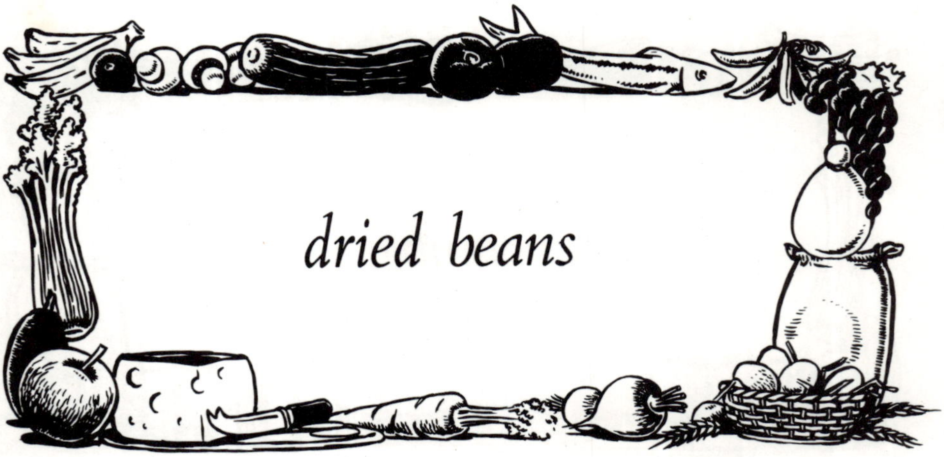

dried beans

Beans are an excellent source of protein, iron, calcium and magnesium. Buy beans in dried form and store in air-tight containers. They do not keep indefinitely, but if stored correctly they should keep for 6 months to a year.

Always wash beans thoroughly before cooking to remove dust and grit. Beans should be soaked overnight to shorten the cooking time. During soaking the water lost in the drying process is reabsorbed and the beans double in size. Use plenty of water to cook beans. They should always be covered. Any beans left out of the water will become dry and inedible.

minestrone stew

serves 8–10

100g haricot or red kidney beans
2 cloves garlic crushed
1 medium sized leek chopped
2 cups vegetable or chicken stock or water
100g carrot chunks
100g celery chunks
100g zucchini chunks
100g potato chunks peeled
10 green beans topped and tailed and cut into 4
10 medium sized mushrooms cut in half (optional)
2x425g tins salt free tomatoes
1 teaspoon basil
1 teaspoon marjoram
3 tablespoons cornflour
¼ cup water
¼ cup fresh parsley finely chopped
2 tablespoons fresh chives finely chopped

Soak beans overnight. Drain and cover with water. Bring to the boil, reduce heat and simmer for 1–1½ hours or until beans are tender. Drain.

Place garlic, leek and stock in a medium sized casserole or saucepan. Simmer for 10 minutes. Add remaining ingredients except the cornflour, water, parsley and chives. Cook until vegetables are tender.

Mix cornflour with water. Add to the casserole. Bring to the boil and stir to thicken. Reduce heat. Add beans and herbs. Serve with wholemeal noodles or wholemeal toast.

chilli bean salad on wholemeal pita breads

serves 6

6 small wholemeal pita breads
shredded lettuce
6–8 medium tomatoes
1 quantity chilli beans warm or cold (see page 71)

Top pita breads with shredded lettuce. Cut tomatoes into quarters, remove seeds and cut each quarter into 4 thin strips. Make a circle of strips around the outside edge of pita breads. Top with chilli bean mixture. Garnish, if desired, with thin strips of carrot and alfalfa sprouts.

chilli con carne beans vegetarian style

serves 10–12

2 cups red kidney beans
2 small onions
2 cloves garlic crushed
300g carrots
400g green beans
2 small red capsicums
1x300ml tin salt free tomato juice
2x425g tins salt free tomatoes and juice
1–2 teaspoons chilli powder
½ cup fresh parsley finely chopped

Cover beans with water and soak overnight. Drain. Cover with clean cold water. Bring to the boil, reduce heat and simmer for 1 hour or until beans are tender. Drain and reserve cooking liquid.

Cook onion and garlic in a little water until soft and transparent (approximately 3 minutes). Add vegetables and ½ cup of cooking liquid from the beans. Simmer until vegetables begin to soften. Add tomato juice, tomatoes and chilli powder. Cook gently for 20 minutes. Add beans. Sprinkle over parsley and serve. Serve in a scooped out baked potato. Mash extra potato and pipe on top. Reheat

or

Fill a large scooped out tomato with chilli con carne beans. Cook in a moderately hot oven for 10 minutes or until tomato is soft.

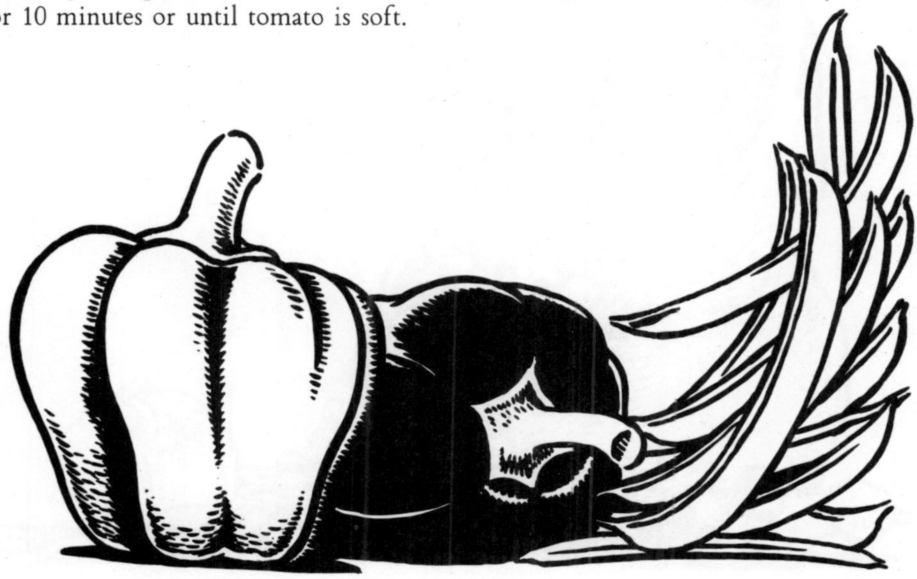

zucchini stuffed with chilli beans

serves 6

3 large zucchini
1 quantity chilli beans warm (see below)
1 cup wholemeal breadcrumbs
1 cup low fat grating cheese

Chilli beans:

100g Adsuki beans
1x425g tin salt free tomatoes
2 small red chillies (for a milder flavour use a medium sized red capsicum)
2 spring onions finely chopped
1 clove garlic crushed
¼ teaspoon cumin
¼ teaspoon dried oregano
2 tablespoons salt free tomato paste

Soak beans overnight. Drain and discard any beans that have not absorbed the water. Place in a clean saucepan and cover with water. Bring to the boil. Reduce heat, cover and simmer for 1–1½ hours or until beans are tender. Drain. Chop tomatoes and add to pan with juice. Add very finely chopped chillies, spring onions, garlic, spices and tomato paste. Cook for 15 minutes, stirring occasionally.

Cut zucchini in half lengthwise and scoop out seeds and some flesh. Chop flesh finely and add to tomato mixture. Cook a further 5 minutes. Add beans and keep hot.

Lightly steam zucchini until just tender. Fill zucchini with bean mixture. Place in a non stick casserole. Sprinkle over breadcrumbs and the cheese. Cook in a hot oven for 15 minutes. Serve.

dried fruits

prune bars

makes approximately 24

⅔ cup prunes finely chopped
⅓ cup dried apple finely chopped
1 tablespoon sunflower seeds
1 tablespoon sesame seeds toasted
½ cup rolled oats or rolled wheat flakes
½ cup raw bran
1 cup almonds in their skins
½ cup skim milk powder
1 tablespoon vanilla essence
⅓ cup unsweetened orange juice
2 teaspoons lemon zest finely grated

Combine the first 8 ingredients in a food processor and chop roughly. Add vanilla and orange juice to bind. Add lemon zest. Line a 30x20cm slab tin with foil and press mixture into it. Refrigerate for at least 4 hours. Cut into bars.

chewy fruits

Keep dried apricots, peaches, nectarines, apples, bananas and pears in the freezer.

These make a delicious cold chewy treat for children.

golly wolly banana logs

200g dried banana
100g dried apple
1 cup almonds in their skins
1 cup rolled oats
½ cup shredded coconut
3 tablespoons apple juice concentrate
squeeze of lemon or orange juice
extra shredded coconut

Chop banana and apple roughly in a food processor using the steel blade. Add all ingredients except apple juice concentrate. Process until mixture resembles large breadcrumbs.

Add apple juice concentrate. Process lightly. If the mixture is too dry add a squeeze of lemon or orange juice. Mixture will come together in your hands. Roll into log shapes approximately 4-6cm long. Roll in coconut. Store in the freezer for a chewy texture.

basic oat munchies

makes 20–24

2 cups rolled oats
1 cup wholemeal plain flour
1 teaspoon baking powder
½ teaspoon mixed spice
½ teaspoon cinnamon
1 cup mixed dried fruit medley
¼ cup sunflower seeds
½ cup apple juice concentrate
¼ cup cold compressed almond oil
2 egg whites lightly beaten

Combine the first 7 ingredients and mix well. Stir through the apple juice concentrate and oil. Add egg whites and mix well. Line a 20x30cm slice tin with non stick baking paper. Press mixture into tin and flatten down. Mark into 12 bars with sharp knife. Cook at 200°C for 15–20 minutes. Cool. Cut into bars.

muesli fruit bars

makes 12

2 cups rolled oats
1 cup wholemeal plain flour (80%)
1 teaspoon baking powder
½–1 teaspoon mixed spice
½ teaspoon cinnamon
2 cups dried fruit medley (apricots, apples, pears and sultanas)
½ cup sunflower seeds
½ cup apple juice concentrate
¼ cup cold compressed oil
3 egg whites lightly beaten

Place apricots, orange juice and apple juice concentrate in a saucepan and simmer over low heat for 10 minutes. Do not drain. Remove saucepan from heat. Blend in skim milk powder. Add almonds, sesame seeds, grated orange rind, sultanas and coconut. Mix well and leave to cool slightly.

Roll mixture into a log shape and roll in toasted coconut. Roll up in foil and keep in refrigerator. Cut into rounds as required. Wrap individual pieces in coloured cellophane to use as gifts.

apricot and almond health chews

½ cup dried apricots chopped
¼ cup unsweetened orange juice
2 tablespoons apple juice concentrate
½ cup skim milk powder
¼ cup whole almonds roughly chopped
1 tablespoon sesame seeds toasted
1 teaspoon orange zest grated
½ cup sultanas or currants
¼ cup shredded coconut
extra shredded coconut toasted

Combine the first 7 ingredients in a large bowl. Combine the last 3 ingredients. Mix together until mixture is well combined and sticky. Place dessertspoonful mounds on a non stick baking sheet. Bake at 200°C for 10–15 minutes until golden.

currant munchies

makes 20

2 cups rolled oats
1 cup wholemeal plain flour
1 teaspoon baking powder
1½ teaspoons mixed spice
1 cup currants
2 teaspoons lemon zest finely grated
½ cup apple juice concentrate
¼ cup cold compressed oil
2 egg whites lightly beaten

Follow instructions for basic munchies opposite.

date and apple munchies

makes 20–24

2 cups rolled oats
1 cup wholemeal plain flour
1 teaspoon baking powder
½ teaspoon mixed spice
½ teaspoon nutmeg
½ cup dates finely chopped
½ cup dried apple finely chopped
½ cup apple juice concentrate
¼ cup cold compressed oil
2 egg whites lightly beaten

Follow instructions for basic munchies opposite.

apricot nibbles

makes approximately 20

¾ cup dried apricots
¾ cup coconut shredded
1 teaspoon lemon zest grated
1 teaspoon orange zest grated
1 tablespoon unsweetened orange juice
extra shredded coconut toasted

Cover apricots with boiling water and stand 10 minutes. Drain off liquid. Mince apricots and mix in lightly with the coconut in a food blender. Add remaining ingredients. Knead until well blended. If mixture is too dry add more orange juice. If mixture is too wet add more coconut. Shape into small balls and roll in toasted coconut. Refrigerate.

muesli munchies

makes 20–24

2 cups toasted muesli sugar free and salt free
1 cup wholemeal plain flour
1 teaspoon baking powder
1 teaspoon cinnamon
¾ cup sultanas
½ cup apple juice concentrate
¼ cup cold compressed oil
2 egg whites lightly beaten

Follow instructions for basic munchies opposite.

drinks

Most commercially sold fizzy drinks are loaded with sugar and artificial flavourings and colourings. You can make your own fizzy drink at home by mixing 1 part unsweetened natural fruit juices, which are high in vitamin C, with 2 parts mineral or soda water.

Try orange, pineapple, apple, dark grape, grapefruit, orange and mango, and your own combinations of any of these juices. Serve with ice blocks.

To make clear ice blocks, fill ice block tray with hot water. Add pieces of fresh fruit such as strawberries, cherries, pineapple pieces or grapes to the ice block tray and freeze.

For a special occasion with older children, choose long-stemmed glasses. Place a strawberry, piece of pineapple and a slice of fresh apricot or other suitable fruit at the base of the glass. Pour in just enough sparkling apple juice to cover fruit. Place in the freezer and freeze. To serve, top up with well chilled sparkling apple juice. Decorate drink glasses with slices of lemon, strawberry or kebabs of fruit, cocktail stirrers or paper parasols to add colour and interest. A teenager's cocktail!

Juices:
Freshly squeezed or extracted fruit and vegetable juices are by far the most delicious and nutritious drinks. Some fruits and vegetables which cannot be squeezed can be placed in a juice extractor which extracts the juice from the pulp by a rotary crushing action.

The pulp remaining is mainly fruit fibre and can be added to the juice for complete food value. Fruit pulp can also be added to cakes for extra moisture or vegetable pulp to soups for added flavour. However, do not store the pulp. It loses its colour, taste and nutritional value.

Fruits to juice:
oranges
grapefruit
lemons
apples
watermelon
pineapple
grapes
apricots

Vegetables to juice:
carrot
celery
tomato
cucumber

Combinations:
orange and pineapple
orange and grapefruit
apple and carrot
apple and celery
tomato and cucumber

All citrus juices combine well.

1 cup skim milk or soy or goat's milk
½–¾ cup fresh fruit puree (see below)
¼ teaspoon vanilla or orange essence (optional)
and/or 1 tablespoon apple juice concentrate or 4 fresh dates
2 ice blocks

Combine all ingredients in a blender and blend until frothy and smooth:

Fruits:
Use bananas, pears, apricots, peaches, strawberries, raspberries, blueberries or kiwi fruit.

peppermint refresher

serves 1

½ cup cold peppermint tea
½ cup ice cold soda water
ice blocks
peppermint or fresh mint leaves to garnish

Add soda to peppermint tea and garnish with ice blocks and leaves.

pink fizz

serves 1

½ cup watermelon flesh
1 cup ice cold soda water

Remove seeds of watermelon and push the flesh through a fine sieve. Add soda to watermelon and serve with pink straws and a pink parasol.

eggs

Although a whole egg is excellent food value, the yolk of the egg contains fat and cholesterol.

It is this fat and cholesterol building up in our bodies over a period of years which leads to the arterial plaque in our arteries, making us candidates for heart disease and other associated problems in later years.

If we realise this at an early age and only include such foods occasionally (for example, 1 egg per week or less) then excessive fat and cholesterol build-up may be avoided in later years.

These two egg recipes are an excellent source of food value because they not only contain a small quantity of egg, but a lot of vegetable and grain content as well.

I suggest you alternate these recipes once a week or once a fortnight for an easy Sunday evening meal.

1 egg yolk vegetable omelette

serves 1

1 egg
1 extra egg white
½ cup soy or skim milk
50g carrot grated
50g zucchini grated
50g fresh tomato chopped
50g low fat grating cheese grated

Beat eggs with soy milk until light and fluffy. Fold in vegetables. Pour onto a hot lightly greased non stick frypan. Spread vegetables evenly over omelette. Sprinkle cheese over the top. Cook for a few minutes until the omelette begins to firm on the bottom then place under a griller until cheese and top brown. Fold in half and remove from pan. Serve with a salad.

egg combination rice

serves 6

3 whole eggs
¼ cup soy milk
1 medium sized onion
1 clove garlic crushed
½ teaspoon fresh ginger finely chopped
125g red capsicum diced
125g green capsicum diced
125g carrots diced
125g zucchini diced
1 tablespoon water
pinch cumin
pinch coriander
pinch chilli powder
1 tablespoon low salt soy sauce
4 cups cooked rice

Beat eggs and soy milk until light and fluffy. Pour onto a hot, lightly greased non stick frypan. Turn to cook the other side. It is cooked when firm and a yellow colour. Do not allow to brown. Remove from pan and chop up into small pieces. Clean away egg from pan.

Add onion, garlic, ginger, vegetables and water to pan. Toss vegetables well and add spices. Cook for 3 minutes. Turn heat up to high. Add rice, a cup at a time, and mix to combine vegetables evenly. Keep turning, using an egg lifter so the rice does not stick to the bottom of the pan. Add egg and mix through rice. When heated through, rice is ready to eat.

overleaf 1: breads: back — spicy fruit buns (page 47); pumpkin wholemeal scones (page 117); cheesy bread sticks (page 50); herb bread muffins (page 120); front — herb scones (page 121)

overleaf 2: Chinese corn and vegetable combination (page 66); Chinese spring rolls (page 65)

overleaf 3: beef and vegetable family pie (page 38); mushroom mini pies (page 103); 1 egg yolk vegetable omelette (page 78); tomato cheese quiche (page 134)

opposite: fruit salad — honeydew melon chunks, pineapple chunks, purple and green grapes, blueberries, dark grape juice (page 85); apples baked with fruit filling (page 27); lemon 'meringue' pie (page 97)

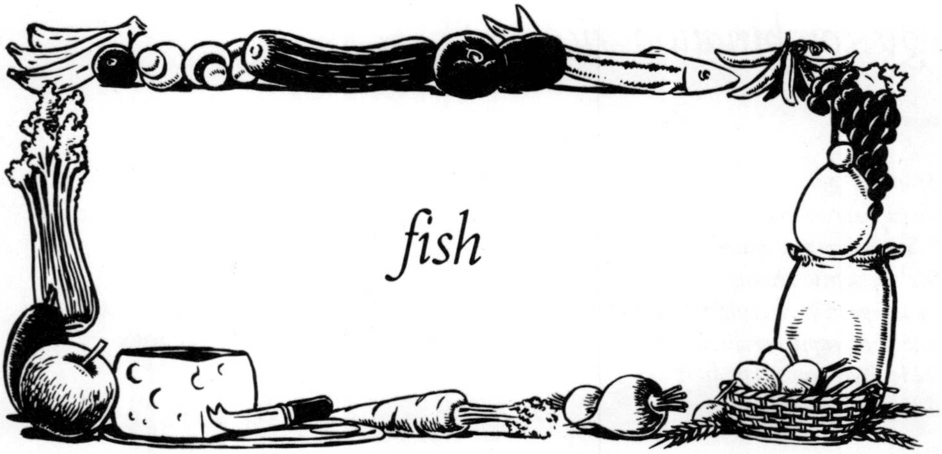

fish

fish and chips

Fish:
Choose low fat varieties of fish (allow 50–90g per person)
wholemeal flour
fine wholemeal breadcrumbs
egg white
lemon juice

Squeeze lemon juice over fish. Dip fish in flour and shake off excess. Dip in lightly beaten egg white and press down in breadcrumbs until both sides are evenly coated. Shake off excess. Refrigerate fish in crumbs for at least 2 hours prior to cooking. Cook in a lightly greased non stick pan until both sides are golden brown (approximately 3 minutes each side

or

Place in a lightly floured oven bag, seal and cook at 200°C for 15–20 minutes.

Fish cooks quickly, so do not overcook. Fish is cooked when an inserted knife flakes the flesh easily.

To help fish retain moisture and to add flavour, fish fillets can be marinated in fruit juices with fresh herbs, garlic, ginger, tomato paste, white wine, non fat yoghurt and spices. Try your own combinations.

Place fish from marinade into breadcrumbs and cook as above.

Chips:
Cut peeled or unpeeled potatoes into chips. Place on a non stick baking tray. Cook at 250°C for 15 minutes or until browned. Non fat yoghurt can be brushed over the chips to help in the browning process.

Add flavour by sprinkling over garlic powder, onion powder, cayenne pepper or finely ground skim milk cheese with herbs.

Potatoes can be peeled and cut into chips and quickly sealed in plastic bags to freeze. Use as required and cook as above.

cheesy topped fish dish

serves 5

5 fillets Blue Grenadier or other suitable fish
1 cup salt free tomatoes and juice pureed
½ cup non fat yoghurt
2 teaspoons low salt soy sauce
2 teaspoons white wine vinegar
½–1 teaspoon curry powder
1 clove garlic finely chopped
½ cup spring onions finely chopped
½ cup celery finely chopped
½ teaspoon tarragon
½ teaspoon basil
2 tablespoons fresh parsley finely chopped

Topping:
1 cup breadcrumbs
½ teaspoon basil
1 celery stalk finely chopped
½ cup low fat grating cheese

Place onion, garlic and celery on the base of an oblong casserole. Sprinkle with parsley. Place fish fillets on top of parsley. Mix together tomato puree, yoghurt, soy sauce, vinegar, curry, tarragon and basil. Pour over the fish. Cover and stand for approximately 1 hour.

Mix topping ingredients together. Spread over top of fish. Cook at 180°C for 35–40 minutes. Serve with a selection of steamed vegetables or brown rice and tossed salad.

tuna and vegetable pie

serves 6

Pie crust:
6 slices wholemeal bread

Filling:
1 medium sized onion finely diced
1½ cups low fat evaporated skim milk or soy milk
1 tablespoon salt free tomato paste
1 cup tuna water packed, salt free
1 cup carrot grated
1 cup celery finely diced
1 small green capsicum finely diced
¼ cup fresh parsley finely chopped
2 tablespoons fresh chives finely chopped
4 tablespoons cornflour
½ cup water

Crumble the bread into fine breadcrumbs. Lightly grease a small pie dish. Reserve ¾ cup breadcrumbs for topping. Place breadcrumbs in pie dish and spread over base and sides evenly. Firm down with fingers and palm of your hand. Cook at 200°C for 10 minutes. Remove from oven. Turn oven up to 220°C.

While pie crust is cooking, cook onion in 1 tablespoon water for 3 minutes or until transparent. Add milk and simmer 2 minutes. Stir in tomato paste. Add tuna, carrot, celery and capsicum. Simmer, covered, for 5 minutes. Add parsley and chives.

Mix the cornflour with the water to make a thin paste. Stir this through the tuna mixture and cook for 2 minutes stirring continuously. Cool slightly. Pour into pie crust. Sprinkle with remaining breadcrumbs. Cook at 220°C for 10 minutes. Turn oven down to 200°C and cook for further 20 minutes. Serve with a tossed salad or lightly steamed vegetables.

salmon bake

serves 6–8

Base:

1 cup cooked brown rice
400g broccoli cooked and pureed

Combine rice and broccoli and mix well. Spoon onto a shallow lightly greased ovenproof dish.

Filling:

1x450g tin salmon salt free packed in water
1 medium sized onion finely chopped
500ml soy milk
¼ cup cornflour
1 teaspoon hot low salt mustard
1 medium sized red capsicum
1 medium sized green capsicum

Cook onion for 3 minutes in 2 tablespoons water. Add soy milk, keeping ¼ cup aside. Blend this with the cornflour to make a paste. Add to heated soy milk, stirring until it thickens. Cook gently for 2 minutes, stirring continuously. Add salmon and mustard and mix well. Remove from heat.

Chop capsicums finely and cook in a small amount of water for 2 minutes to soften. Drain. Add to salmon. Pour over the base.

Topping:

6 slices wholemeal bread made into breadcrumbs
125g low fat grating cheese
¼ cup fresh parsley finely chopped

Combine topping ingredients and mix well. Spoon over top of salmon. Cook at 190°C for 20–30 minutes until top browns.

fish vegetable bundles

serves 6

6 fish fillets
julienne strips of carrot, zucchini, green beans, cucumber, red and green capsicums (approximately 8–10 strips per fillet)
1 cup non fat yoghurt
½ cup non fat grating cheese grated
1 cup wholemeal breadcrumbs
2 tablespoons fresh parsley finely chopped
2 tablespoons fresh chives finely chopped

Roll fish fillets to flatten slightly. Place combination of julienne vegetables in centre of fillet with ends of vegetable visible at either side. Roll up. Place in a shallow lightly greased ovenproof dish with seam side down. Pour over yoghurt and sprinkle with cheese.

Combine breadcrumbs, parsley and chives. Sprinkle over fish. Cover with foil. Cook at 180°C for 20–30 minutes or until fish is tender. Remove foil for the last few minutes to brown and crisp breadcrumbs. Serve with salad or steamed vegetables and small steamed potatoes.

fruit jellies

Fruit jellies are a delicious treat any time of the day. They are easily made from freshly squeezed fruit juices or bottled, unsweetened fruit juices. For interesting flavours try different juice combinations and add some freshly chopped fruit to the jelly just before it sets. I have used agar powder to set the fruit to make a jelly. You could easily substitute gelatine as the setting ingredient. If using agar the setting time is greatly reduced.

apple mint jelly

serves 4

2 cups unsweetened apple juice
1 teaspoon agar powder
1–2 teaspoons fresh mint or spearmint finely chopped

Boil 1 teaspoon of agar with 1 cup apple juice for 3 minutes or until agar has dissolved. Stir briskly into remaining cold juice. Stir continuously for 3 minutes. Stir through the mint. Refrigerate to set.

fruit cocktail jelly

serves 4

2 cups unsweetened fruit cocktail juice (combination of orange, apple, mango and passionfruit)
1 teaspoon agar powder
1 tablespoon passionfruit pulp

Boil 1 teaspoon agar with 1 cup juice for 3 minutes or until agar is thoroughly dissolved. Stir briskly into remaining cold juice. Stir continuously for 3 minutes. Stir in passionfruit pulp. Refrigerate to set. It will set very quickly.

blueberry grape jelly

serves 6

2 cups dark unsweetened grape juice
2 teaspoons agar powder
2 cups blueberries fresh or frozen

Boil 2 teaspoons agar with 1 cup juice and blueberries for 3 minutes or until agar has dissolved. Stir briskly into remaining cold juice. Stir continuously for 3 minutes. Refrigerate to set.

pineapple jelly

serves 4–6

¾ cup unsweetened pineapple juice
1 cup water
1 tin unsweetened pineapple pieces
1½ teaspoons agar powder

Boil 1½ teaspoons agar with 1 cup water for 3 minutes or until agar has dissolved. Stir briskly into the pineapple juice. Stir continuously for 3 minutes. Chop pineapple pieces roughly. Fold pineapple through just before jelly sets.

rainbow wobbly jellies

serves 4–6

Orange:
2 cups unsweetened orange juice
1 teaspoon agar

Purple:
2 cups unsweetened dark grape juice
1 teaspoon agar

Clear:
2 cups clear unsweetened apple juice
1 teaspoon agar

Make up jellies separately using basic jelly-making instructions. Pour into separate containers. Leave jelly to set. Run a fork through the jellies and break up. Spoon into parfait glasses, alternating colours.

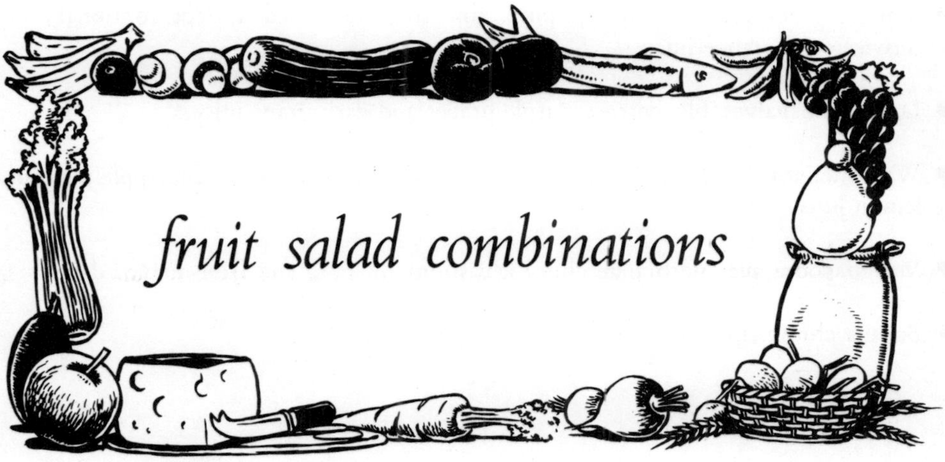

fruit salad combinations

Fruit salad can be a nutritious finish to a meal, served for breakfast or as a snack meal. It need never become boring if you change the combinations of the fruit and soak it in a little juice. Serve plain, with home made ice cream, custard or non fat yoghurt.

- Orange segments, grapefruit segments, pineapple chunks, passionfruit pulp and orange juice.
- Strawberries, watermelon balls and sparkling apple juice.
- Cantaloupe balls, honeydew melon balls, green grapes, grated fresh ginger root and natural, unsweetened pear juice.
- Banana chunks, pineapple chunks, apple chunks, purple grapes, lemon juice and natural, unsweetened apple juice.
- Honeydew melon chunks, cantaloupe chunks, pineapple chunks, purple and green grapes, blueberries and dark grape juice.
- Orange chunks, apple chunks, pear chunks, pineapple chunks, strips of dried apricot and orange or apple juice.
- Apricot halves, peach pieces, nectarine pieces and apricot nectar.
- Pineapple chunks, banana chunks, passionfruit pulp and unsweetened pineapple juice.
- Strawberries, kiwi fruit chunks, green grapes, zest of orange and lemon and unsweetened orange juice.
- Bananas sliced, kiwi fruit sliced, pineapple wedges, orange segments, water chestnuts thinly sliced, glazed cherries (rinsed to remove sugar) and lemon and orange juice.

- Mango, pineapple, passionfruit pulp, fine strips of dried apricot (optional) and unsweetened orange juice.
- Dark plum halves, blueberries, purple grapes and dark grape juice.
- Watermelon balls, honeydew melon balls, cantaloupe balls, sparkling apple juice and lemon juice.
- Mango, pineapple and orange chunks, passionfruit pulp and fresh halved dates.
- Banana chunks, passionfruit pulp and fresh halved dates.

grapes

Grapes are a source of vitamins C and A, calcium, phosphorus, iron, potassium and thiamin. They are low in sodium and high in natural sugar.

frozen grape kebab

Thread large or small green and purple grapes onto a wooden skewer. Place in the freezer until frozen. This makes a refreshing treat on a hot day, although it is not suitable for very small children.

grapes and melon balls

Combine equal quantities of green and purple grapes with honeydew melon, cantaloupe and watermelon balls. Use a melon baller to scoop round flesh shapes. These look delicious presented in a glass bowl. Squeeze over fresh lemon, lime or orange juice.

Decorate with long thin strips of orange and lemon rind, with pith removed or cut very thin strips of dry apricot and toss through. Refrigerate. Serve with ice cream or vanilla flavoured non fat yoghurt.

ice-creams

An ice cream maker will make the best non fat ice cream without added sugar, egg yolks and artificial flavourings and colourings. There are many different designs now available so it is necessary to choose wisely and follow the manufacturer's instructions on ice cream freezing times.

The cheapest or the most expensive machine is not necessarily the best machine for you. Consider how many members of your family enjoy ice cream treats, and how often you would use the machine. Add up how much money you would spend over a 12 month period on commercial ice cream, then decide on whether an ice cream maker is a worthwhile investment for your family.

It is worth noting that in 1984 and 1985 Australia produced 280 million litres of ice cream and related ice cream confectionary. The population of Australia at that same period was 15½ million. This means that approximately 18 litres of ice cream per head per year was produced!

I personally think that the greatest advantage of such an investment is knowing what ingredients your ice cream contains. The endless varieties of ice cream and all the wonderful flavours are just an added bonus!

Making ice cream without an ice cream maker:

- All ingredients used should be ice cold.
- All equipment used should be well chilled. Place in freezer for at least 15 minutes prior to using.
- Pour ice cream into well chilled metal freezing containers.
- To avoid ice cream texture becoming icy rather than creamy, you will need to rebeat it several times, just as icicles begin to appear around the edges again, making sure that all equipment is well chilled.
- This ice cream does not store well as it becomes rock hard. Make small batches and eat as required.
- Should ice cream become too hard, place in a chilled blender or food processor and quickly blend to a creamy texture. Eat immediately.

rich creamy custard ice cream

serves 10

4 cups skim milk
¼ cup cornflour
1 tablespoon orange zest
2 teaspoons vanilla essence
½ cup apple juice concentrate
1 cup non fat yoghurt or extra skim milk

Place 3 cups milk in a saucepan and slowly bring to the boil. Combine cornflour, orange zest and vanilla with 1 cup milk. Stir to make a smooth paste. Add to milk and stir continuously for 2–3 minutes until the mixture thickens. Remove from heat. Add apple juice concentrate and fold through. Add yoghurt or milk and stir again until smooth. Cool until just warm. Pour into ice cream maker following freezing instructions.

light carob ice cream

serves 6

1x375ml tin ice cold evaporated skim milk
or
3 cups non fat yoghurt
1 tablespoon carob powder
2 teaspoons vanilla essence
2 tablespoons apple juice concentrate

If using milk, beat until thick and at least doubled in size. Combine carob, vanilla and apple juice concentrate. Add to milk or yoghurt. If using yoghurt fold through. Do not beat or you will lose the creamy texture. Pour into ice cream maker following freezing instructions.

rich creamy carob ice cream

serves 6

1x375ml tin ice cold evaporated skim milk
¼ cup unsweetened carob powder
¼ cup apple juice concentrate
2 teaspoons vanilla essence

Beat milk until thick and at least doubled in size. Combine carob, apple juice concentrate and vanilla to make a thick paste. Add this mixture to milk while still beating. Pour into the ice cream maker following freezing instructions.

Variations:
Add 2 tablespoons finely chopped roasted almonds, toasted coconut or finely chopped raisins.

passionfruit ice cream

serves 6

½x375ml tin ice cold evaporated skim milk
1 cup unsweetened fruit juice cocktail (a combination of apple orange, peach and passionfruit juices)
½ teaspoon orange essence
¼ cup apple juice concentrate
2 tablespoons passionfruit pulp

Beat milk until thick and at least doubled in size. Add remaining ingredients while still beating. Pour into ice cream maker following freezing instructions. When ice cream begins to thicken, add passionfruit pulp.

strawberry ice cream

serves 8–10

1x375ml tin ice cold evaporated skim milk
2 teaspoons vanilla essence
1 tablespoon apple juice concentrate
2 punnets strawberries

Beat milk until thick and creamy and at least doubled in size. Add vanilla and apple juice concentrate. Mash 1 punnet of strawberries and cut remaining strawberries in half. Add strawberries. Pour into ice cream maker following freezing instructions.

chunky banana ice cream

serves 8–10

1x375ml tin ice cold evaporated skim milk
3 teaspoons vanilla essence
2 tablespoons lemon juice
4 bananas

Beat milk until thick and creamy and at least doubled in size. Add vanilla and lemon juice. Add roughly chopped bananas and beat lightly. Pour into ice cream maker following freezing instructions.

orange flavoured ice cream

serves 6

1x375ml tin ice cold evaporated skim milk
2 teaspoons vanilla essence
1 teaspoon orange essence
¼ cup apple juice concentrate

Beat milk until thick and at least doubled in size. Add remaining ingredients while still beating. Pour into ice cream maker following freezing instructions.

boysenberry ice cream

serves 8

1x300g pack frozen unsweetened boysenberries
2 tablespoons apple juice concentrate
1 teaspoon vanilla essence
or
½ teaspoon orange essence
1½ cups evaporated skim milk
or
1x250ml pack soy milk

Crush berries with the palm of your hand. Place in a blender or food processor. Process until icy. Pour in remaining ingredients. Beat until at least doubled in size. Pour into ice cream maker following freezing instructions.

pineapple flavoured ice cream

serves 10–12

1x375ml tin ice cold evaporated skim milk
2 teaspoons vanilla essence
2 cups unsweetened pineapple juice
½ cup apple juice concentrate

Beat milk until thick and at least doubled in size. Add remaining ingredients while still beating. Pour into ice cream maker following freezing instructions.

kiwi fruit

Kiwi fruit is an excellent source of vitamins C and A, iron, phosphorus, sodium and potassium.

kiwi fruit in an egg cup

serves 1

Place a chilled kiwi fruit in an egg cup. Remove top. Provide a spoon to scoop the flesh away from the fuzzy outer skin.

kiwi fruit jelly

serves 4

4 kiwi fruit
⅔ cup clear unsweetened apple juice
2 tablespoons apple juice concentrate
1 tablespoon gelatine
½ cup boiling water

Dissolve gelatine in boiling water and leave to cool slightly. Slice kiwi fruit and place in a small serving bowl. Add apple juice and apple juice concentrate to the dissolved gelatine. Stir well. Pour over the kiwi fruit. Refrigerate until set.

Variation:
Puree the kiwi fruit and mix all ingredients together thoroughly.

kiwi fruit ice

serves 2

2 kiwi fruit

Remove outer fuzzy skin and cut fruit into 8 pieces. Freeze for at least 4–8 hours. Remove from freezer and stand for a few minutes. Place in a food processor and process until thick and creamy. Mould into 2 round balls and serve with strawberries or chunks of fresh pineapple.

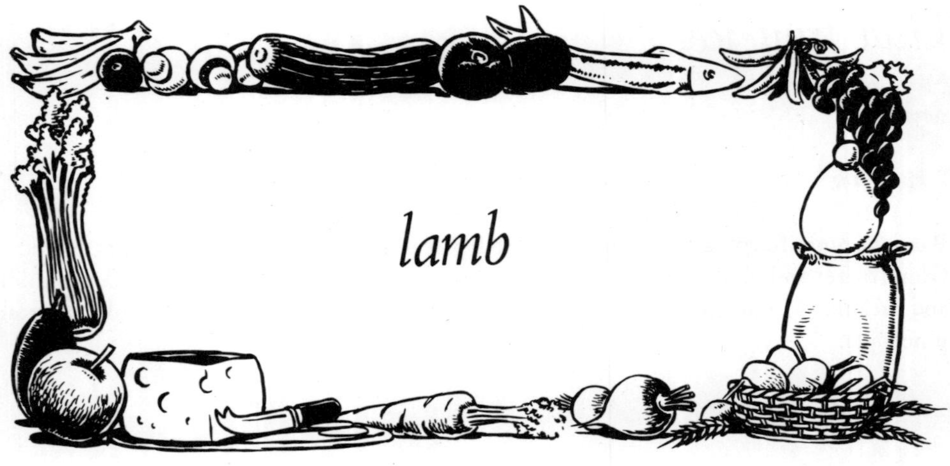

lamb

spicy lamb and rice

serves 10–12

2 cups uncooked brown rice
1kg lamb meat with visible fat removed
2 medium sized onions finely diced
½–1 teaspoon coriander powder
½ teaspoon ginger powder
½–1 teaspoon cumin
1 cup beef or vegetable stock
2 green peppers cut into small pieces
2 carrots cut into small pieces
2 cups sultanas
2 celery stalks cut into small pieces

Cook rice in boiling water until tender. Mince lamb and remove sinew. Cook onion for 3 minutes or until soft in a small amount of water. Add meat and spices. Simmer, covered, for 30 minutes.

Break meat up into small pieces as it cooks so it retains its minced texture. Add stock as necessary so meat does not dry out. This is a dry dish so avoid adding too much liquid. Add vegetables and sultanas and cook, covered, for 10 minutes. Fold through the cooked drained rice. Serve in crisp lettuce cups.

opposite: salads — back — orange, cucumber and mint salad; middle — Hawaiian coleslaw (page 53); vegetable coleslaw (page 51); apple salad (page 28)

centre spread: back, left to right — Chicken casserole with snow peas (page 62); brown rice; chicken sweet and sour (page 63); front, left to right — chicken chausseur served with brown rice (page 61); chicken chausseur casserole (page 61)

far overleaf: fruit jellies, back — rainbow wobbly jellies (page 84); middle, left to right — lemon parfaits (page 98); carob mousse (page 55); front, left to right — blueberry grape jelly (page 84); fruit cocktail jelly (page 83)

Mexican lamb balls with sweet potatoes and peas

serves 6

400g lamb with visible fat removed
1 medium sized onion finely diced
2 cups wholemeal breadcrumbs
1¾ cups water

Sauce:
1 medium sized onion diced
2 cloves garlic crushed (optional)
½ teaspoon fresh ginger finely chopped
1x400g tin salt free tomatoes in juice pureed
¼ cup salt free tomato paste
1 cup stock (liquid in which meatballs are cooked)
2 tablespoons low salt soy sauce
1 large red capsicum
4 spring onions
2 stalks celery

Mince lamb and mix with onion and breadcrumbs. Roll mixture into small balls (approximately 20). Place in a shallow pan. Cover with water and bring to the boil. Place lid on and turn heat down to simmer. Cook for approximately 30 minutes. Remove meatballs and retain stock.

Place onion, garlic and ginger in a saucepan. Add a little stock. Place lid on and cook for 3 minutes. Add tomatoes, tomato paste, stock and soy sauce. Cook for 10 minutes. Cut capsicum in half. Remove seeds and cut into long strips. Cut onions and celery into small diagonal pieces.

Place meatballs into a casserole dish and add vegetables. Pour over sauce. Place lid on casserole. Cook 30 minutes at 200–220°C. Serve with 2 medium sized sweet potatoes and ½ cup green peas per person.

To cook sweet potatoes, peel and cut into cubes. Simmer until just tender.

lamb curry

serves 10

1kg boned lamb with visible fat removed
1 large onion
1 teaspoon fresh ginger finely chopped
1 cup carrot chopped
1 cup beans chopped
1 cup celery chopped
1 cup green capsicum chopped
1 cup sultanas

Sauce:
3 cups lamb stock or water
3 tablespoons salt free tomato paste
3 tablespoons cornflour
2 teaspoons curry powder
½ teaspoons cumin
zest of ½ lemon cut into thin strips

Mince lamb, removing any sinew. Stir fry lamb (in 3 lots) to seal meat and lightly brown. Remove from pan and set aside. Stir fry onion and ginger until onion is transparent (approximately 2–3 minutes). Add vegetables and sultanas, tossing to combine. Add meat and combined sauce ingredients. Place in a casserole dish. Cook at 190°C for 1 hour.

lamb roast dinner with vegetables

1–2kg boned piece of shoulder lamb with visible fat removed

Stuffing:
1¾ cups wholemeal breadcrumbs
10 dried apricots finely chopped
1 apple grated
¼ cup fresh parsley finely chopped
½ teaspoon sage
wholemeal flour
ground black pepper

Gravy:
2 tablespoons low salt tomato paste
arrowroot

Combine all stuffing ingredients, mix well and fill cavity in meat. Secure ends with fine meat skewers. Roll meat in wholemeal flour, seasoned with ground black pepper and shake off excess. Place in an oven bag. Cook at 220°C for 25 minutes per ½kg.

When cooked, pour off excess juice and remove fat. Add tomato paste and water. Allow ¼ cup water per person. Simmer and thicken with arrowroot (combine arrowroot with water to make a paste).

Serve with any of the following vegetables: Potatoes, pumpkin, peas, brussel sprouts, cauliflower, carrots, beans, spinach, parsnip, corn, zucchini, cabbage, sweet potatoes, yellow squash, broccoli, tomatoes or red and green capsicums.

Vegetables can be steamed or baked. To bake vegetables, place on a non stick baking tray or place in an oven bag. Follow cooking instructions on oven bag packet.

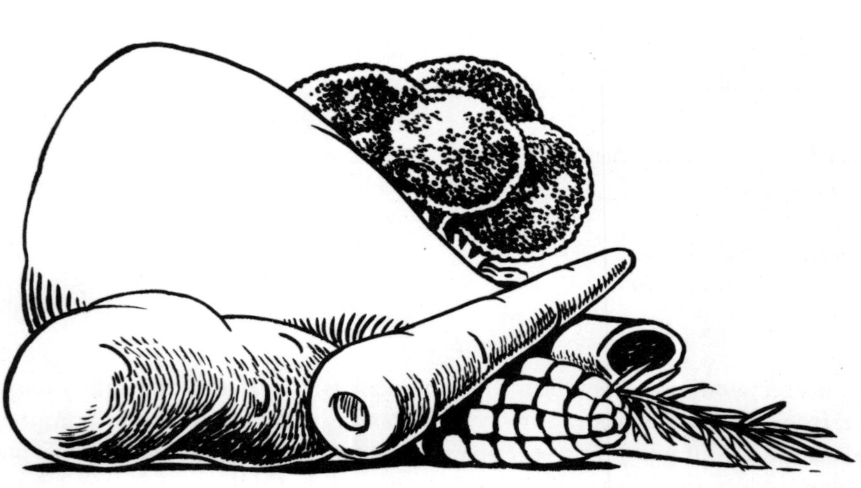

lemons

lemon 'meringue' pie

serves 8

Pastry:

1 cup wholemeal plain flour (80%)
1 cup rolled oats
¼ cup cold compressed oil
2 tablespoons apple juice concentrate
4 tablespoons lemon juice

Combine all ingredients in a food processor and process until pastry binds together. Roll out to fit a small fluted pie dish. Cook at 220°C for 10–15 minutes. Cool.

Lemon filling:

¾ cup lemon juice
½ cup apple juice concentrate
zest of 1 orange (approximately 1 tablespoon)
zest of 1 lemon (approximately 1 tablespoon)
1¼ cups water
½ cup cornflour

Place the first 4 ingredients plus 1 cup water in a small saucepan and bring to the boil. Combine ¼ cup water with cornflour and make into a paste. Stir into lemon mixture stirring continuously as it boils and thickens. Cook for 2 minutes. Cool slightly. Pour into base and leave to set.

The lemon filling should be quite cold and firm before making the meringue topping.

Meringue topping:

4 egg whites
100g almonds finely ground
1 teaspoon vanilla essence
2 tablespoons apple juice concentrate

Beat egg whites until stiff peaks form. Add all other ingredients separately, mixing well after each addition. Spoon over lemon filling. Cook at 200°C for 10–15 minutes or until top has browned.

This pie should be kept out of the refrigerator for best flavour. Serve with non fat frozen yoghurt or home made ice cream.

lemon parfaits

serves 4–6

1 cup lemon sauce (*see* Pancake party *page 107*)
1 cup ice cold evaporated skim milk
1 teaspoon gelatine
2 tablespoons boiling water

Dissolve gelatine in boiling water and set aside to cool. Beat milk until thick and at least doubled in size. Beat in the lemon sauce. If lemon sauce has been refrigerated you will need to heat it slightly to soften the texture and ensure easier combining. Pour into parfait glasses and refrigerate. Garnish with green and purple grapes and a mint leaf.

lemon pear sorbet

serves 8–10

1x825 tin unsweetened pears and juice
¼ cup apple juice concentrate
4 tablespoons lemon juice

Puree all ingredients. Pour into an ice cream maker and follow freezing instructions. Serve in sugar free ice cream cones. Garnish with a piece of fresh fruit such as a strawberry or kiwi fruit.

homemade lemonade

serves 6

½ cup lemon juice (approximately 2½ lemons)
¼ cup apple juice concentrate
½ teaspoon orange essence
soda or mineral water
ice blocks

Mix the first 3 ingredients together. Fill glass with ice blocks. Add 2 tablespoons lemon mixture. Top up with mineral or soda water. To increase quantities slightly reduce apple juice concentrate. That is, 2 cups lemon juice to ¾ cup apple juice concentrate.

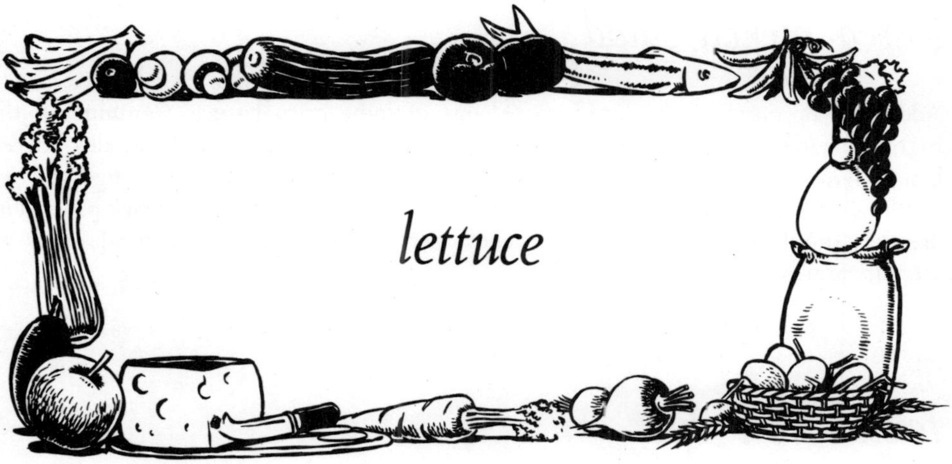

lettuce

Lettuce leaves are a good source of vitamin A, potassium, thiamin, calcium, phosphorous, iron and some vitamin C. The darker outside leaves contain the most vitamin A and iron, so wash thoroughly and include these in a tossed salad.

tossed lettuce salad 1

A tossed salad is an excellent addition to the daily diet. Nutrient value is retained when food is raw and a salad of raw ingredients is not only nutritious but very flavoursome, high in essential fibre and low in calories.

Lettuce is the basic ingredient of a tossed salad. A combination of any of the following can be added to it:

- celery chunks
- green or red capsicum chunks or strips
- carrot chunks or thin strips
- zucchini chunks or thin rounds
- cherry tomatoes or tomato slices
- alfalfa sprouts
- mung bean sprouts
- snow peas

Crisping lettuce and other vegetables:
Tear lettuce leaves away from the stalk. Wash leaves in cold water and drain thoroughly. Store in a plastic bag in the crisper or wrap in a tea towel until required.

To make vegetables such as carrots, celery, cabbage, capsicum, zucchini and snow peas crisp, soak in iced water for at least 10 minutes. Drain thoroughly and store as for lettuce until required. Add dressing of your choice just before serving.

Only dressings from *Taste of Life* and *More Taste of Life* are recommended.

tossed lettuce salad 2

Choose one variety of lettuce and break into small pieces in a bowl. Add a squeeze of lemon juice, a splash of white wine vinegar and some finely chopped fresh herbs. Alternatively, combine different varieties of lettuce such as butter lettuce, mignonette, cos and crisphead lettuces and dress as above.

tossed mixed salad

Add three or more of the listed ingredients to some crisp lettuce. Combine all the ingredients in a large salad bowl. Add some fresh finely chopped herbs like parsley, chives, basil, thyme or tarragon. You could add a squeeze of lemon juice or orange juice or combine lemon juice, tomato paste, some white wine vinegar and ground black paper. The dressing should be a pouring consistency. Serve salad chilled as a meal or as an accompaniment to other food.

lettuce roll ups

These are parcels of goodies wrapped up tightly in lettuce leaves.

Use combinations of grated raw vegetables. Add freshly chopped herbs and a dash of salad dressing or wrap up leftover foods. Use cold spaghetti, vegetable sauce, vegetable rice salad, tabbouleh or rice coleslaw.

Use two lettuce leaves and lie flat. Place food in the centre. Fold one edge over food. Fold both sides over and roll up. Lay seam side down.

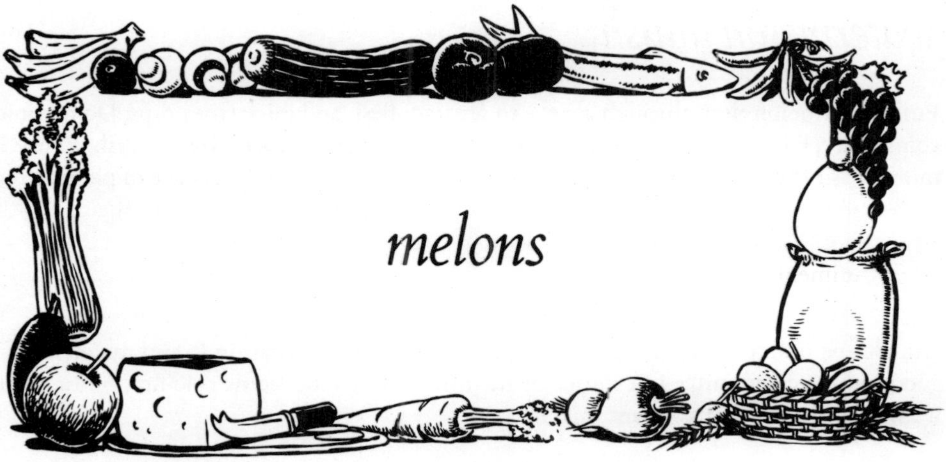

melons

Watermelon is approximately 90 per cent water. When ripe the skin should be a rich deep green.

watermelon basket with fresh fruits

1 large watermelon
a selection of fruits to make up a large fresh fruit salad such as strawberries, pineapple, apples, bananas, grapes, pears, melons, oranges, plums, nectarines, mandarins, peaches, kiwi fruit and passionfruit pulp.

Cut away shaded areas as shown. Scoop out flesh leaving just a hint of red on the inside of watermelon. Chop up some of the watermelon flesh, remove pips and add to the fruit salad. Store leftover watermelon flesh in freezer for watermelon juice or watermelon mush (see over). Make up fresh fruit salad by cutting fruits into chunks. Fill basket with fruits and chill.

Watermelon birthday basket:
Cut small grooves into the basket handle so birthday candles will sit upright. Light the candles and serve fruit salad in coloured cups with coloured spoons.

watermelon juice

Push watermelon flesh through a sieve to separate flesh and black pips. Place watermelon pulp into a juicer or blender. Process until liquid. Chill well. Add just a squeeze of fresh lemon juice or a small amount of fresh ginger juice. To juice fresh ginger, peel and cut up finely. Press through a garlic press to extract juice. Serve over ice blocks with a slice of lemon or combine ½ mineral water and ½ juice for a fizzy red drink. This is very refreshing on a hot day.

watermelon mush

Push watermelon flesh through a sieve to separate flesh and juice from pips. Do not juice completely, but combine juice evenly with flesh. Pour into a metal freezer dish. Every 15 minutes stir the icy mush until it freezes evenly. Do not over freeze. Serve in plastic mugs with a spoon.

Cantaloupe is an excellent source of vitamin A, is high in vitamin C and magnesium, a good source of sodium, a fair source of thiamin and includes some calcium, phosphorus, iron, potassium, riboflavin and niacin.

cantaloupe berry basket

serves 3

1 cantaloupe
2–3 cups mixed berries such as boysenberries, blueberries, raspberries, loganberries, blackberries or strawberries

Cut cantaloupe into quarters. Remove seeds and scoop out the flesh to make a basket-like hollow. Use a sharp knife to carefully remove the flesh from one quarter, leaving approximately 1cm orange flesh. Cut up the flesh into pieces and give to children to nibble on while you make these fun baskets.

Cut the outer skin into three long strips which will become the basket handles. Attach these to either end of remaining pieces of cantaloupe using toothpicks. Wash berries and drain. Fill baskets. Serve with home made ice cream or non fat yoghurt.

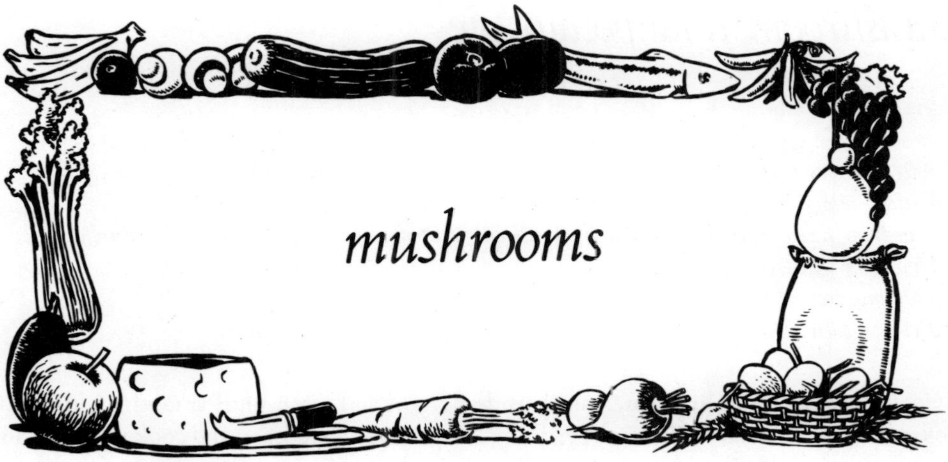

mushrooms

mushroom mini pies

makes 6

6 small foil pie plates
6 slices wholemeal bread
100g mushrooms finely chopped
150g zucchini finely grated
100g fresh tomato finely chopped
2 tablespoons fresh parsley finely chopped
1 teaspoon oregano
1 teaspoon basil
3 egg whites
½ cup non fat yoghurt
100g low fat grating cheese grated

Lightly grease foil pie plates. Roll bread out flat using a rolling pin. Use scissors to cut out a round to fit pie plate. Press into pie plates and trim edges with scissors.

Combine mushrooms, zucchini, tomato, parsley and spices. Beat egg whites and add yoghurt. Fold in cheese and add to vegetables. Spoon into cases. Use the bread scraps to make breadcrumbs. Sprinkle breadcrumbs over pies. Cook at 220°C for 15 minutes and then turn oven down to 200°C and cook for a further 15 minutes. Serve hot or cold.

mushroom caps

serves 6–12

12 large mushrooms, stems removed
2 tablespoons mashed potato for each mushroom
1 tablespoon grated low fat grating cheese for each mushroom
2 tablespoons finely ground wholemeal breadcrumbs for each mushroom

Place mushrooms top down on a lightly greased non stick baking tray. Fill each mushroom with potato. Top with cheese. Sprinkle over breadcrumbs and firm down. Cook at 220°C for 8–10 minutes. Serve with salad or to nibble on.

mushroom and potato pie

serves 4–6

900g potatoes peeled and cubed
4 sticks celery finely chopped
1 medium sized onion peeled and finely diced
1 medium sized carrot grated
400g mushrooms thinly sliced
2 cloves garlic crushed
2 tablespoons cornflour
200ml skim milk
2 tablespoons fresh parsley finely chopped
1 teaspoon thyme
2 teaspoons lemon juice
pinch cayenne pepper

Cook potatoes in boiling water until tender. Drain and mash until smooth. Add a little skim milk if necessary. Place celery, onion and garlic in a saucepan and cook until soft and transparent. Add 2 tablespoons water to avoid sticking to base of saucepan. Add mushrooms and cook for a further 10 minutes.

Blend cornflour and milk and stir into the mushrooms. Add parsley, thyme, lemon juice and cayenne pepper. Simmer for 5 minutes. Pour mixture into a lightly greased ovenproof dish. Spoon over mashed potatoes and spread evenly. Cook at 190°C for 20 minutes or until potato begins to turn brown.

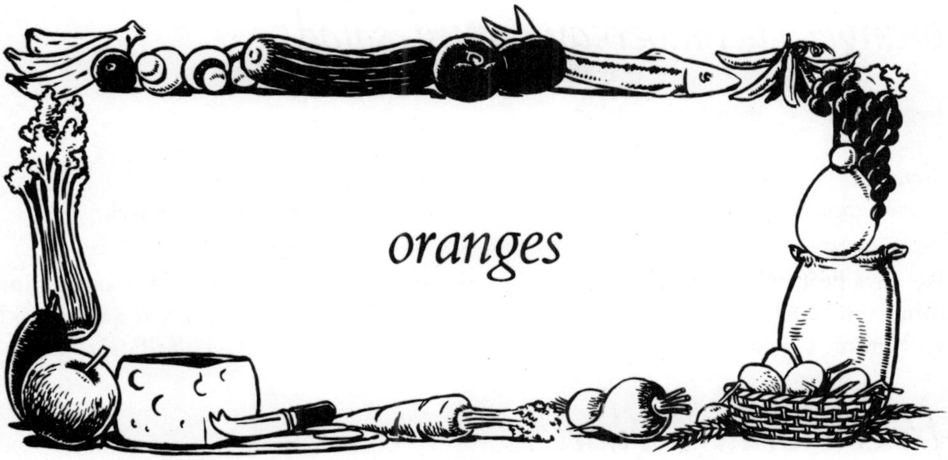

oranges

Oranges are an excellent source of vitamin C and natural fibre.

frozen orange cups

Use thick skinned oranges. Remove tops from oranges. Using a sharp knife, ease the orange flesh away from the outer skin. Use fingers or a knife to remove orange flesh pieces. Cut away any pith and remove pips. Cut orange into small pieces.

Combine orange flesh with some passionfruit pulp and other chopped fresh fruit (such as pineapple, apple or mandarin). Fill orange cups with fruit. Top up with freshly squeezed orange juice or unsweetened pure orange juice. Place on a small tray and freeze until just mushy. If left for too long they will become rock hard and too hard for children to manage.

To make sure oranges sit flat while freezing, cut a small slice across the bottom of the orange, taking care not to make a hole in the orange.

orange, cantaloupe and passionfruit cups

serves 4

4 oranges
¼–½ small cantaloupe
4 passionfruit
½ cup unsweetened orange juice

Remove tops from oranges and carefully scoop out orange flesh. Remove white pith and pips and chop orange finely. Cut up cantaloupe finely. Scoop pulp from passionfruit. Combine fruits and orange juice. Spoon into orange cups and chill.

orange, cucumber and mint salad

serves 6–8

3 oranges
1 small cucumber
½ cup apple cider vinegar
2 tablespoons fresh mint finely chopped

Remove peel and pith from orange and cut into thin rounds. Peel cucumber and cut into thin rounds. Alternate layers of orange and cucumber. Pour over vinegar and sprinkle with mint. Cover and chill. Serve on a bed of lettuce leaves or on alfalfa sprouts.

frozen orange quarters

Cut oranges into 4 pieces. Remove pith and visible pips. Freeze until hard.

This beats a sugar loaded, preservative added and artificially coloured icypole on a hot day and is much better for you.

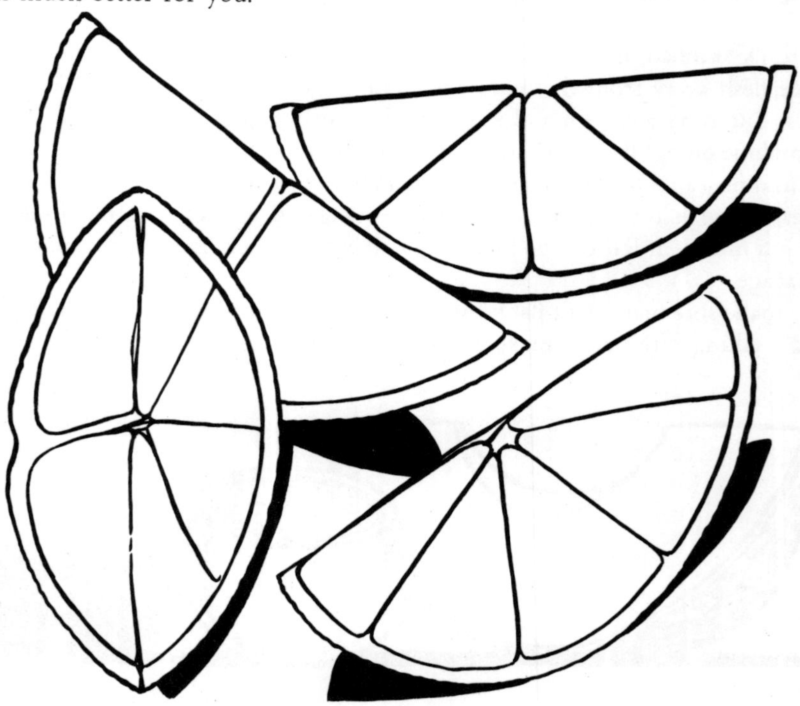

pancake party

makes 16 pancakes

Pancakes:

4 cups water
3 cups rolled oats
2 cups wholemeal plain flour
2 teaspoons baking powder
½ cup apple juice concentrate
2 teaspoons vanilla essence
4 egg whites

Combine all ingredients except egg whites in a food blender or processor. (It may be easier to divide quantity into 2 and do in separate batches.) Process until smooth. Beat egg whites until stiff peaks form. Fold egg whites through the mixture.

Cook pancakes on a hot non stick flat pan. Approximately ½ cup of mixture makes 1 pancake. As air bubbles appear turn over and brown other side. Move pancake mixture around to spread for an even texture. Keep pancakes hot in the oven by placing between two pieces of foil on a baking tray. Set oven at approximately 100–150°C. When ready to serve, fold pancakes in half. Top with a scoop of home made ice cream and a topping of your choice, or with fresh fruit such as sliced strawberries, mashed bananas, pineapple or kiwi fruit.

Or

Make a pancake stack. Pour sauce over the top and let it dribble down over the edges.

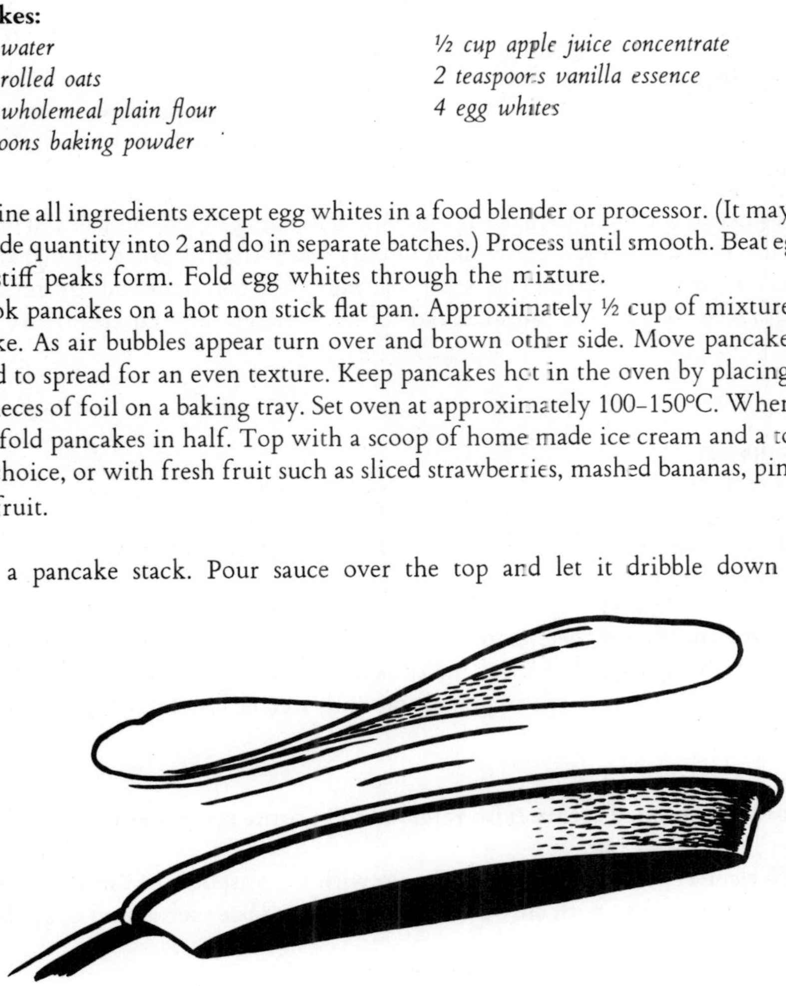

Lemon topping:

¾ cup lemon juice
½ cup apple juice concentrate
½ teaspoon orange essence
rind of 1 orange grated (optional)
1¼ cups water
¼ cup cornflour

Combine first 4 ingredients plus 1 cup of water in a small saucepan. Combine ¼ cup water and cornflour to make a paste. Slowly bring lemon mixture to the boil. Add cornflour mixture and stir continuously until sauce thickens. Remove from heat and cool slightly. Pour over home made ice cream and pancakes.

Blueberry topping:

2 cups unsweetened natural pear juice
⅓ cup apple juice concentrate
450g blueberries, fresh or frozen
1 tablespoon lemon juice
¼ cup cornflour

Mix ¼ cup pear juice with cornflour to make a paste. Combine other ingredients in a small saucepan and slowly bring to the boil. Add cornflour and stir continuously until sauce thickens. Remove from heat and cool slightly. Pour over home made ice cream and pancakes.

Banana topping:

1 banana per pancake
1½ cups unsweetened orange, pear or apple juice
1 tablespoon lemon juice
1 tablespoon apple juice concentrate
1–2 teaspoons cornflour

Add a little juice to cornflour to make a paste. Add remaining liquid to a pan and bring to the boil. Turn heat down and simmer until liquid reduces slightly. Slice bananas and add to the sauce. Bring to the boil and cook for 1 minute. Add cornflour and stir until sauce boils and thickens. Pour over pancakes and top with ricotta low fat cream (see *cherry topping*).

Cherry topping:

500g stoned cherries
1 cup unsweetened orange juice
½ cup apple juice concentrate
½ teaspoon orange essence
zest of 1 lemon
1 tablespoon lemon juice
1 teaspoon (scant) agar

Place all ingredients except cherries in a saucepan. Bring to the boil and simmer for 10–15 minutes to dissolve agar. Add cherries and cook a further 5 minutes. Remove from heat and cool slightly. Pour over pancakes and top with ricotta low fat whipped cream.

Ricotta low fat whipped cream (also referred to in some recipes as low fat whipped cream):

Beat low fat ricotta cheese until smooth. Flavour with 1–2 teaspoons of vanilla essence and thin to desired consistency with unsweetened natural fruit juice such as pear or apple juice, or apricot nectar.

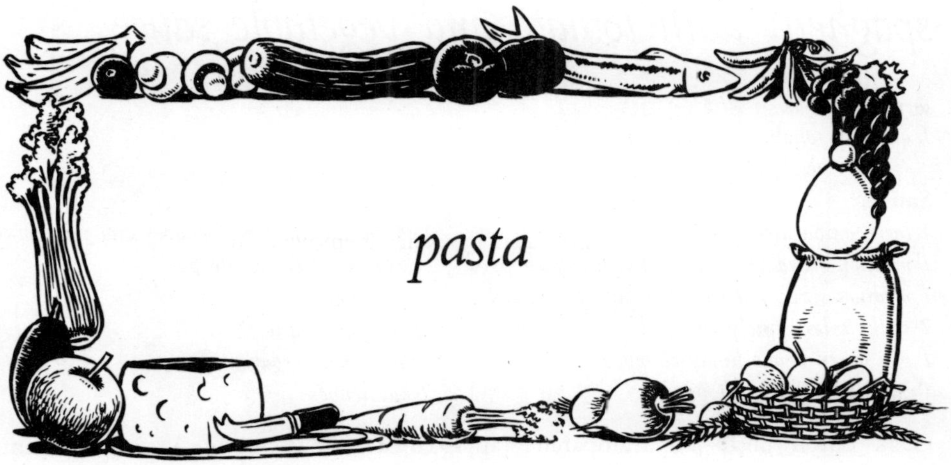

pasta

spaghetti and meatballs

serves 6

1 quantity wholemeal spaghetti

Meatballs:

250g fat free beef or veal finely minced
1 onion finely minced
1 cup wholemeal breadcrumbs
1 granny smith apple grated

Combine all ingredients and roll into very small balls. Place in a shallow pan in approximately 3cm water. Bring to the boil. turn heat down and simmer, covered, for approximately 8 minutes. Remove from pan and drain

Tomato sauce:

1 onion diced
1 small green capsicum
1 small red capsicum
1x425g tin salt free tomatoes pureed
½ teaspoon oregano
¼ cup fresh parsley finely chopped
1 cup water
2 tablespoons salt free tomato paste
½ teaspoon basil

Cook onion and capsicum in a little water to soften (approximately 3 minutes). Add tomatoes and water. Bring to the boil. Add tomato paste, basil and oregano. Cook for 20 minutes. Sauce should boil and thicken and slightly reduce. Add meatballs to sauce and heat through.

Boil 2 litres of water while making sauce. Add wholemeal spaghetti and cook until tender. Serve sauce and meatballs over spaghetti and sprinkle with fresh parsley.

spaghetti with tomato and vegetable sauce

serves 6
1 quantity wholemeal spaghetti

Sauce:
1 large onion diced
1 medium sized green capsicum finely chopped
1 medium sized red capsicum finely chopped
2 stalks celery finely chopped
1 cup green beans finely chopped
1 cup carrot finely chopped
1x425g tin salt free tomatoes and juice pureed
¼ cup salt free tomato paste
1 cup water
½ teaspoon basil
½ teaspoon oregano
2 bay leaves

Cook onion until just transparent (approximately 2–3 minutes). Add remaining ingredients. Bring to the boil. Reduce heat and simmer for 30–40 minutes.

Boil 2 litres of water while making sauce. Add wholemeal spaghetti and cook until tender. Serve sauce over cooked spaghetti. Sprinkle with finely chopped parsley or low fat grating cheese or a combination of both.

macaroni with vegetables and cheese topping

serves 6–8

200g wholemeal macaroni or soyaroni noodles
225g carrots diced
255g zucchini diced
4 stalks celery chopped
2 cups vegetable stock or water
2 cups skim milk
¾ cup cornflour
½ cup fresh parsley finely chopped
1 cup low fat grating cheese grated

Cook macaroni in boiling water until tender. Drain. Cook vegetables in stock until tender. Drain and keep liquid. Cool slightly. Add 1½ cups milk and bring to almost boiling. Combine ½ cup milk with cornflour and stir to make a paste. Stir through remaining milk and vegetable stock, stirring continuously until stock thickens.

Add parsley and cheese. Combine vegetables and macaroni in an ovenproof dish. Pour over cheese sauce. Cook at 200°C for 15–20 minutes or until top begins to brown.

Variation:
Top with 1–2 cups wholemeal breadcrumbs.

macaroni cheese

This is a quick and easy snack.
wholemeal macaroni or other noodles such as soyaroni or vegetable noodles

Cook noodles following instructions on the packet. Sprinkle with low fat grating cheese and toss through some finely chopped fresh herbs such as parsley, chives and basil.

For each person allow 1 cup of cooked noodles for 2 tablespoons of finely grated low fat grating cheese and 1 tablespoon of finely chopped fresh herbs.

pineapple

pineapple fruit boat

serves 1–2

1 small fresh pineapple
some fresh strawberries
some banana chopped
some jonathon or delicious apple roughly chopped
1 passionfruit

Cut pineapple, including green foliage, in half. Cut out pineapple flesh and remove the core. Chop up pineapple flesh finely. Combine all other ingredients and toss well in the passionfruit pulp. Spoon into the pineapple shell and refrigerate well. Delicious served with frozen non fat yoghurt.

pineapple and mint dip

makes approximately 1½ cups

1 cup low fat cottage cheese
½ cup fresh pineapple very finely chopped
2 teaspoons fresh mint very finely chopped

Combine all ingredients and mix well. Refrigerate and chill. Serve with vegetable crudites, wholewheat biscuits or wholemeal bread, or spoon into crisp lettuce leaves.

overleaf: pancake stack with blueberry topping and homemade ice cream (page 108); pancakes with lemon sauce and homemade ice cream (page 108)
opposite: casseroles: back — tuna and vegetable pie (page 81); centre — zucchini moussaka (page 138); salmon bake (page 82)

pizza party

pizza party for 15–20

makes approximately 30 slices

5 large pita breads

or

1kg pack wholemeal salt free bread mix

Make up as instructed and add a teaspoon oregano to dry flour (optional). Let bread dough sit for 10–15 minutes. Divide into 5 pieces. Use a rolling pin to roll out to fit 5x30cm round pizza trays or place on large baking trays. Cover and stand for 15 minutes. Top with the following.

Pizza sauce:
makes approximately 5 cups

3 medium sized onions diced
2 cloves garlic crushed
2x400g tins salt free tomatoes pureed
1 cup salt free tomato paste
½ teaspoon basil
1 teaspoon oregano

Cook onions and garlic in a little water until soft. Add remaining ingredients and boil for 5 minutes to thicken. Set aside to cool.

Mushroom pizza:
makes 1

1 cup pizza sauce
200g mushrooms finely chopped
100g low fat grating cheese finely grated

Spread 1 cup pizza sauce over base. Sprinkle over mushrooms and cover with cheese. Cook for 10–15 minutes at 200°C.

Hawaiian pizza:
makes 2

2 cups pizza sauce
150g green capsicum cut into strips
150g red capsicum cut into strips
400g unsweetened pineapple crushed and well drained
100g low fat grating cheese finely grated

Divide ingredients equally between two bases. Spread 1 cup pizza sauce over each base. Add capsicums, pineapple and top with cheese. Cook for 10–15 minutes at 200°C.

Vegetarian delight:
makes 2

2 cups pizza sauce
200g low fat grating cheese finely grated
200g carrots cut into thin rounds and lightly cooked until just soft
200g zucchini cut into thin rounds and lightly cooked until just soft
150g tomato cut into thin round slices

Divide ingredients equally between 2 bases. Spread 1 cup pizza sauce over each base. Sprinkle cheese over pizza base. Place carrot rounds and zucchini rounds over cheese. Top with slices of tomato. Cook for 10–15 minutes at 200°C. Serve with a large tossed salad.

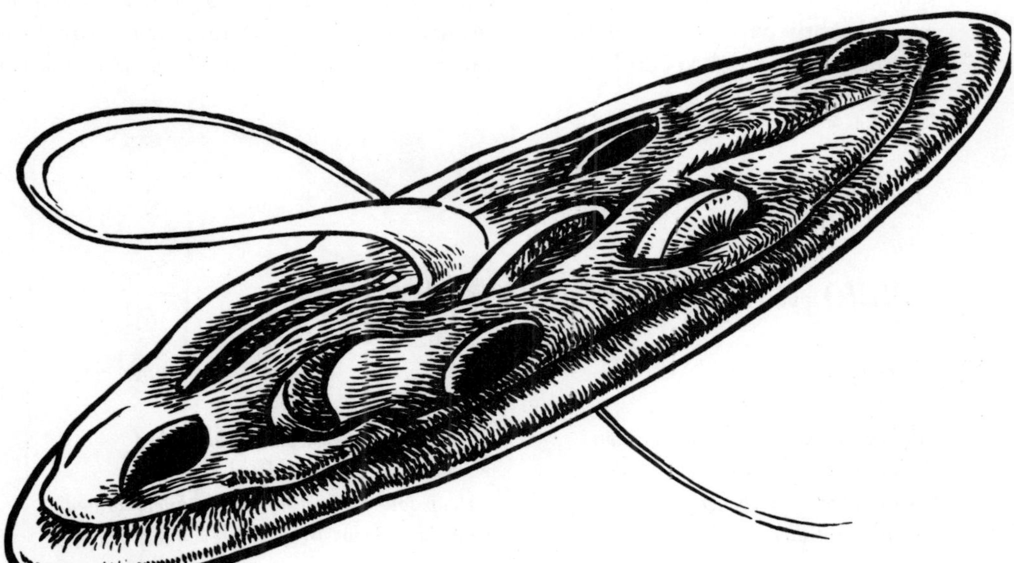

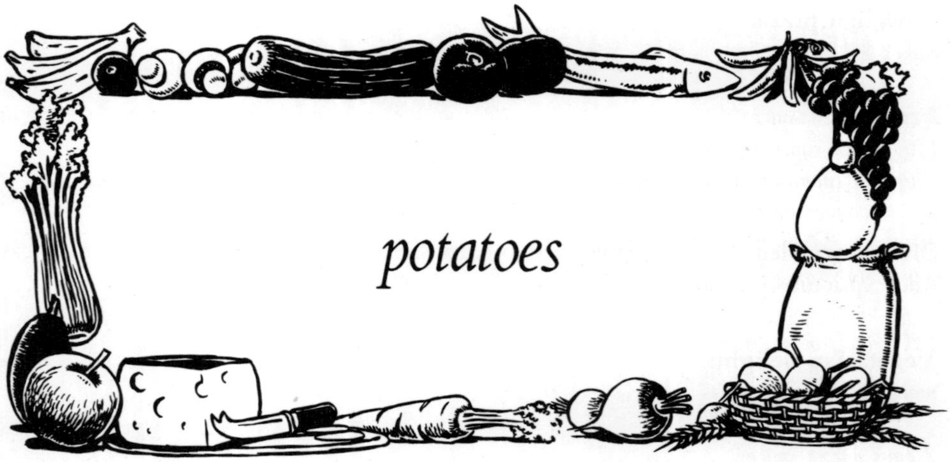

potatoes

potato hunza pie

makes 8–10 slices

6 sheets wholemeal filo pastry
1·25kg potatoes peeled and cubed
1 small bunch spinach cleaned and roughly chopped
1 cup spring onions
1 teaspoon nutmeg
pinch cayenne pepper
2 tablespoons sesame seeds or poppy seeds (optional)

Steam potatoes until tender and drain. Steam spinach until cooked and drain. Combine potatoes, spinach, spring onions, nutmeg and cayenne pepper. Mix well.

Line a large lightly greased pie dish with 4 sheets filo pastry and trim edges. Fill with spinach and potato mixture and spread evenly. Top with 2 sheets of filo pastry and trim edges. Lightly wipe over top with water, using a pastry brush. Sprinkle with sesame seeds or poppy seeds. Cook at 220°C for 10 minutes. Turn heat down to 200°C and cook for a further 20 minutes.

potato whip with vegetables

serves 6–8

All cooked vegetables must be hot.
4 cups potatoes cooked
1 cup green peas cooked
1 cup carrot diced cooked
½ cup green capsicum diced cooked
½ cup red capsicum diced cooked
½ cup low fat grating cheese finely grated
1–2 tablespoons fresh parsley finely chopped

Mash potatoes with a little skim milk to bind. Combine with other ingredients in a piping bag. Pipe interesting mounds onto a child's favourite plate and serve with wholemeal toast fingers.

spinach and potato pasties

makes 12 small pasties

1 quantity wholemeal bread pastry
600g potatoes peeled
10 large silverbeet or 20 spinach leaves finely chopped
8 spring onions finely chopped
150g mushrooms finely chopped
100g low fat grating cheese grated
1 tablespoon salt free tomato paste
1 tablespoon low salt soy sauce
egg white and water

Dice potato and steam until tender. Steam silverbeet or spinach leaves until tender. Drain well. Combine all ingredients except egg white and water. Make up bread dough following packet instructions and cut into 12 portions. Flour a bench, roll dough out and make 12 thin circles.

Divide filling between circles. Place filling on one half of each circle. Fold over remaining half. Wipe edges with egg white and water and press to seal. Place on a non stick baking tray. Bake at 220°C for 10 minutes. Reduce heat to 200°C and cook for a further 20 minutes.

not quite Irish (potato) stew

serves 8–10

1kg potatoes
1 sweet (orange) potato approximately 200g
1 parsnip approximately 125g
2 medium sized carrots approximately 200g
1 zucchini approximately 250g
2 medium sized onions cut into quarters
2 cups frozen peas
3 cups boiling water
1 tablespoon Vecon
1x375ml tin salt free vegetable juice
¼ cup fresh parsley finely chopped
3 tablespoons cornflour
¼ cup water

Prepare all vegetables by peeling and cutting into cubes. Potatoes should be twice the size of other vegetables. Dissolve 1 tablespoon Vecon in 1 cup boiling water. Add all vegetables except peas. Cover with remaining water and vegetable juice. Cover and cook for 40 minutes at approximately 190°C

When vegetables are just tender, add peas, parsley and combined cornflour and water. Cook for 5 minutes more after stew has come to the boil again. Serve with wholemeal bread.

mashed potatoes

Allow one medium sized potato per person.

Simmer peeled potatoes in boiling water under tender. Drain. To make creamy smooth mashed potato, place in a blender or food processor or use an electric hand held beater. Whip until smooth. Add 2 tablespoons low fat grating cheese, 2 tablespoons finely chopped fresh basil or 2 tablespoons finely chopped spring onion.

potato and vegetable pie

serves 6–8

Vegetables:

2 medium sized carrots sliced
1 sweet potato (white or orange) peeled and cubed
1 medium sized zucchini chopped
12 small brussel sprouts
150g cauliflower flowerettes
150g broccoli flowerettes
100g pumpkin peeled and cubed
2 cups peas

Place all vegetables in the top of a steamer and steam for 10–12 minutes or until vegetables are tender.

Gravy:

1 onion peeled and diced
2 cups water or vegetable or chicken stock
1 tablespoon salt free tomato paste or mango chutney (see chicken burger *recipe page 60)*
2 tablespoons cornflour
2 tablespoons water
¼ cup fresh parsley finely chopped

Topping:

3–4 cups hot mashed potato
1 cup low fat grating cheese finely grated

Saute onion in 2 tablespoons stock for 3 minutes. Add remaining stock and tomato paste. Combine cornflour and water to make a paste. Stir cornflour mixture through the stock and bring to the boil. Cook for 2–3 minutes or until gravy thickens. Add parsley.

Place vegetables in a suitable casserole dish. Pour over the gravy. Top with combined potato and cheese. Place in a water bath. Water should come up ½ the side of the casserole dish. Cook at 230°C for 30–40 minutes.

potato cakes

Cut large potatoes into rounds. Lightly steam until just tender. Beat egg white lightly with a little water. Dip potato into mixture and then coat in very fine wholemeal breadcrumbs.

Shake off excess breadcrumbs and place in a floured oven bag and cook at 220°C for 15–20 minutes. Alternatively, lie the potato cakes on a lightly greased foil lined baking tray and cook at 220°C for 10–15 minutes.

Variation:

You could sprinkle the cakes with garlic, onion or celery powder or a little low fat grating cheese.

pumpkin

pumpkin wholemeal scones

makes approximately 10

1 cup wholemeal plain flour (80%)
1 cup unbleached white flour
4 teaspoons baking powder
1 teaspoon nutmeg
2 tablespoons non fat yoghurt
good squeeze of lemon juice (approximately 1 tablespoon)
2 teaspoons apple juice concentrate
½ cup lightly packed raw pumpkin grated
cup skim milk

Sift dry ingredients twice. Add pumpkin and toss in flour to coat well. Add yoghurt, lemon juice and apple juice concentrate. Use a knife to mix together. Slowly add milk, still using the knife to bind ingredients. The mixture will be slightly sticky.

Scrape from bowl onto a lightly floured board. Knead gently. Too much kneading will make the scones heavy. Cut into desired shapes. Place on a non stick scone tray. Cook at 220°C for 10–12 minutes.

quick as a wink pumpkin soup

serves 6–8

800g pumpkin peeled and finely diced
4 cups defatted chicken stock
or
2 cups unsweetened orange juice and 2 cups water
1 medium sized onion
1 teaspoon fresh ginger finely chopped
1 clove garlic crushed (optional)
¼ cup salt free tomato paste
½ teaspoon cumin (optional)

Cook onion, ginger and garlic in 2 tablespoons water for 3 minutes or until transparent. To get the best flavour from onions without cooking in oil, always place lid on saucepan while onions are cooking. Add all other ingredients. Cook for 15–20 minutes or until pumpkin is tender. Puree. Serve with a thin slice of orange and garnish with parsley.

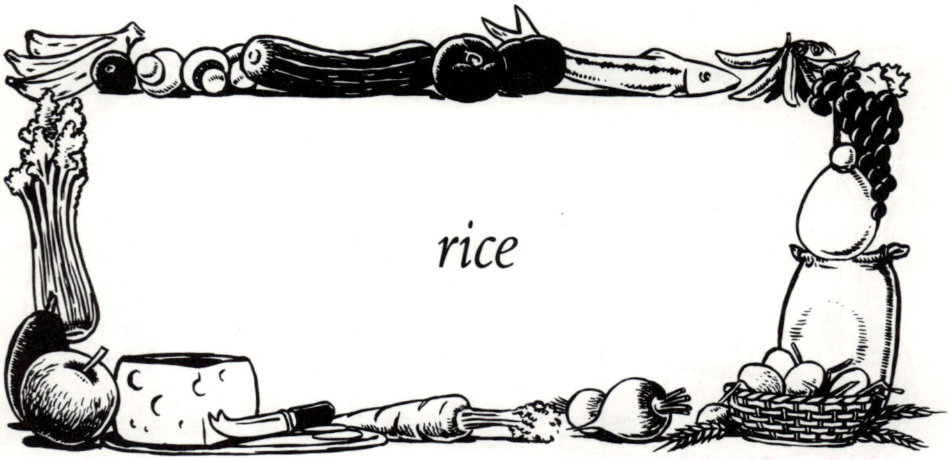

rice

Brown rice is an extremely nutritious food with a wonderful nutty flavour and chewy texture. It is packed with B group vitamins, iron, protein and is a natural complex carbohydrate, because it has not been polished or hulled and still contains its bran casing.
1 cup uncooked brown rice = approximately 3 cups cooked

vegetable rice salad

serves 6

3 cups cooked cold brown rice
1 medium sized carrot diced
2 small celery sticks diced
1 small green capsicum diced
1 small red capsicum diced
¼ cup corn kernels cooked
¼ cup green peas cooked
2 tablespoons fresh parsley finely chopped
2 tablespoons fresh mint finely chopped

Combine vegetables in a container of iced water for 10 minutes. Drain well. Combine all ingredients and toss well.

For a special treat, remove the top from a medium sized tomato. Scoop out inside flesh, pour rice mixture into tomatoes and serve.

tabbouleh rice

serves 6

2 cups cooked brown rice
4 tomatoes peeled, seeded and finely chopped
4 spring onions finely chopped
1 cup fresh parsley finely chopped
1 cup fresh coriander finely chopped
½ cup fresh mint finely chopped
¾ cup garlic vinaigrette

Combine all ingredients and mix well. Chill. Serve in a tomato shell, on crisp lettuce cups, in lettuce leaves rolled up to make a parcel, or in a cucumber boat.

garlic vinaigrette

1 cup apple juice
½ cup white wine vinegar
2 tablespoons lemon juice
2 teaspoons grated lemon rind
4 small cloves garlic peeled and halved

Combine all ingredients n a screw top jar and keep refrigerated. Shake every now and then to combine flavours. Remove garlic before serving. For a stronger garlic flavour, crush it into the dressing.

sweet rice

serves 8

4 cups cooked brown rice
½ cup dried apricots finely chopped
¼ cup currants
¼ cup raisins finely chopped
¼ cup dried apples finely chopped
1 medium sized carrot diced
2 stalks celery diced
1 tablespoon sunflower seeds
1 tablespoon sesame seeds toasted
2 teaspoons orange zest grated
¼ cup unsweetened orange juice

Combine all ingredients and serve immediately.

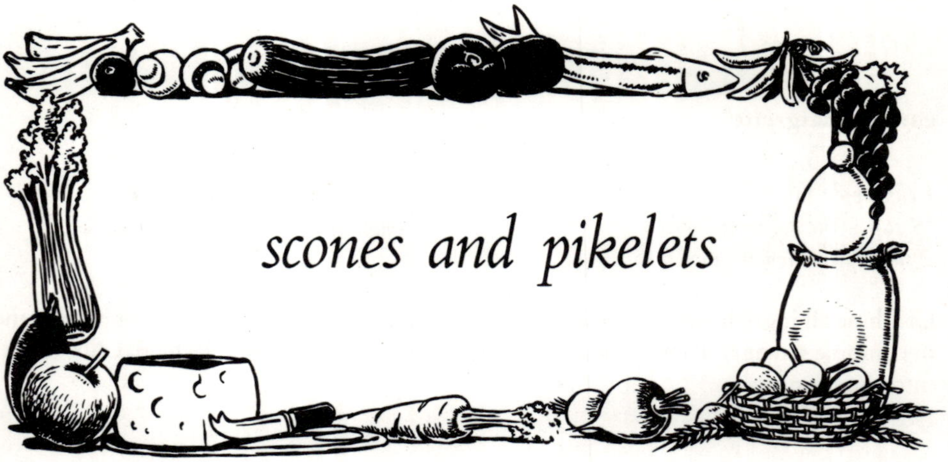

scones and pikelets

herb bread muffins

makes 12

500g wholemeal salt free bread mix
2 teaspoons yeast
2 tablespoons fresh chives, parsley and rosemary finely chopped
320ml luke warm water
2 tablespoons sesame seeds
2 tablespoons sunflower seeds
2 tablespoons poppy seeds

Combine flour, herbs and yeast. Add water and knead to a firm dough (approximately 5–7 minutes). Cover with plastic wrap and leave in a warm position for 10–15 minutes. Divide dough in half and divide each half into 6 equal portions.

Lightly grease a non stick, deep sided muffin tray. Place bread dough into muffin tray, lightly cover with plastic wrap and place in a warm position until doubled in size (approximately 45 minutes). Wipe tops with extra luke warm water and sprinkle over combined seeds.

Cook at 210–220°C for 15–20 minutes or until the tops are crusty. Break open and serve with non fat cottage cheese and salad ingredients, or serve with soups.

cheese and spice pikelets

makes approximately 15

1 cup wholemeal plain flour
2 teaspoons baking powder
½ teaspoon curry powder
½ cup plus 2 tablespoons skim milk
4 tablespoons low fat cheese finely grated

Follow instructions for *basic pikelets*. Serve with slices of tomato and alfalfa sprouts or low fat ricotta cheese with thinly sliced celery.

plain pikelets

makes approximately 15

1 cup wholemeal plain flour (100%)
2 teaspoons baking powder
½ cup skim milk
1 teaspoon vanilla
2 egg whites

Sift flour and baking powder. Add milk and vanilla and beat to make a smooth batter. Add 2 egg whites and beat again until egg whites are absorbed and mixture is smooth.

Place dessertspoons full of mixture on a lightly greased hot pan. As bubbles appear on top of pikelets quickly turn over. Cook until both sides are nicely browned. Top with sliced tomato, low fat cheese, cottage cheese and herbs, sugar free jam or mashed banana.

wholemeal plain scones

makes approximately 12

250g wholemeal plain flour (80%)
4 teaspoons baking powder
2 tablespoons skim milk powder
2 tablespoons apple juice concentrate
good squeeze of lemon juice
1 cup milk or soy milk

Sift dry ingredients. Add apple juice concentrate and lemon juice. Rub into flour using fingers or the blade of a knife. Bind with milk to make a dough. Lightly flour a bench top. Gently knead dough. Too much kneading will make the scones heavy. Cut into shapes. Place side by side on a non stick baking tray. Cook at 200–210°C for 10–15 minutes. Spread with sugar free jam.

herb scones

makes approximately 10

2 cups unbleached white flour
3 teaspoons baking powder
1 tablespoon fresh chives finely chopped
1 tablespoon fresh parsley finely chopped
1 tablespoon fresh rosemary or basil finely chopped
2 tablespoons non fat yoghurt
good squeeze of lemon juice (approximately 1 tablespoon)
cup skim milk or soy milk

Sift flour and baking powder. Add herbs and coat with flour. Add yoghurt and lemon juice and mix through until flour resembles fine breadcrumbs. Add milk and mix through, using a knife. Place scone dough on a lightly floured bench and knead lightly. Cut into desired shapes. Place on a non stick baking tray. Cook at 200°C for 10–15 minutes.

date and cinnamon pikelets

makes approximately 15

1 cup wholemeal plain flour
2 teaspoons baking powder
1 teaspoon cinnamon
10 dates very finely chopped
½ cup skim milk
1 teaspoon vanilla
2 egg whites

Follow instructions for *plain pikelets* recipe on page 121.

simple sandwiches

Sandwiches are an excellent choice for snack food, lunch boxes and main meals. On cold days, pop them under a griller to lightly toast.

Try some of these fillings between some wholesome grain or wholemeal varieties of bread:

- Natex spread with low fat grating cheese, grated carrot, finely sliced celery, finely shredded lettuce, alfalfa sprouts, minced chicken or flaked cold fish.
- Grated carrot with currants, grated cheese, finely chopped red or green capsicum, mung bean sprouts, minced chicken, minced lamb, minced beef, unsweetened crushed pineapple or salt free water packed salmon or tuna.
- Shredded lettuce with chopped egg white, tomato slices, tomato and cucumber slices, grated raw beetroot, minced chicken, minced cold beef or salt free water packed salmon or tuna.
- Tomato with thinly sliced grated zucchini, sprouts or cucumber slices.
- Mashed corn with alfalfa sprouts, finely shredded lettuce, minced chicken or finely sliced celery.
- Mashed banana with sultanas, raisins, currants, grated apple or low fat cottage cheese.
- Low fat cottage cheese with grated carrot, minced chicken, capsicum, dried fruits or mashed banana.

leftover foods for sandwich fillings

spaghetti with spaghetti sauce
baked beans
leftover casseroles
pizza sauce
chilli bean sauce
beef and beans

Spread bread with Natex spread, grated cheese, cottage cheese and top with leftover foods. Use for sandwiches or pop under the griller to lightly toast.

sandwich filling accompaniments

Low fat cottage cheese.

Low fat cottage cheese with fresh or dried herbs.

Mayonnaise:
makes 2 cups

¾ cup low fat evaporated milk
¼ cup apple juice concentrate
2 teaspoons dijon mustard
½ cup wine vinegar

Place ingredients in a screw top jar and shake well. Store in refrigerator. Shake well before each use.

Date and apple chutney:
4 medium sized cooking apples peeled, cored and grated
500g dates seeded and chopped
2 onions finely chopped
1 cup raisins, sultanas or apricots
1 teaspoon chilli powder
2 cups unsweetened orange juice
6 whole cloves
¼ teaspoon ground allspice
1½ cups wine or cider vinegar

Place all ingredients in a large saucepan and bring slowly to the boil over a low heat. Simmer, stirring occasionally for 1 hour or until mixture is of a thick, soft consistency. Spoon into hot sterilised jars and seal when cold. Store in the refrigerator. The flavour will improve if left for at least a week before using.

This is an excellent savoury spread for sandwiches, or can be used as a dip for vegetable and fruit platters, or as a chutney with chicken and fish vegetable loaves.

Tomato chutney spread:
makes 4 litres (approximately)

4 large onions peeled and diced
3kg ripe tomatoes peeled and chopped
6 large granny smith apples
3 cloves garlic crushed
4 cups cider vinegar
250g sultanas
1 cup raisins
1 teaspoon allspice
1 teaspoon mace
1 teaspoon cloves
1 teaspoon chilli powder
1 cup unsweetened orange juice

Combine all ingredients in a large saucepan. Bring to the boil. Boil for 1 hour uncovered, stirring frequently. Remove from heat. Pour into warm bottles. Process in usual method. Once opened, keep refrigerated.
Suggested uses: Piza base, sandwich spread, salad dressing.

Mango chutney (see page 60).

sandwich spreads

Apple spread:

220g dried apples
3 cups unsweetened pineapple juice
½ lemon
2 teaspoons lemon rind
2 teaspoons cinnamon

Combine all ingredients in a large saucepan and simmer over gentle heat until apples are soft. Puree the mixture in a blender and pour into sterilised jars. When cool, seal and store in the refrigerator.

Apricot fruit spread:

125g dried apricots
90g dried apples
60g raisins
3½ cups unsweetened orange juice

Combine all ingredients in a large saucepan and simmer over gentle heat until fruit is soft. Puree the mixture in a blender and pour into sterilised jars. When cool, seal and store in the refrigerator.

Chicken spread:

1 cup minced cooked chicken
1 tablespoon mild onion grated
1 tablespoon fresh parsley finely chopped
1 cup blanched almonds minced
3 tablespoons mayonnaise (see page 78)
pinch dried thyme
1 teaspoon lemon juice

Place all ingredients in a food processor and blend well until smooth. Pour into a small pot and refrigerate. Serve with wholemeal toast fingers or fresh wholemeal bread.

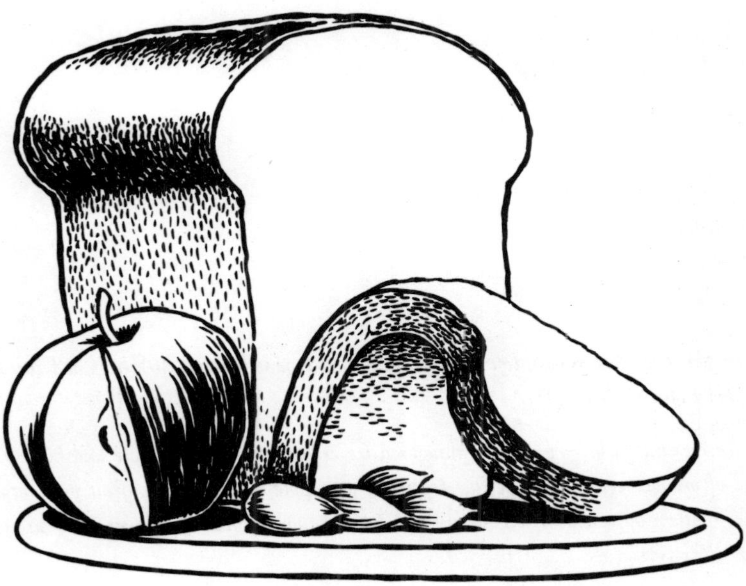

Salmon and cucumber spread:

1 small tin water packed salmon drained
½ cucumber peeled and seeded
½ small capsicum seeded
lemon juice to taste
paprika to taste
fresh parsley finely chopped (optional)

Place all ingredients except parsley in a food processor and blend well until smooth. Pour into a small pot and refrigerate. Parsley can be folded through before pouring into pot if desired.

Serve with wholemeal toast triangles or wholewheat crackers.

Savoury spread:

250g ripe tomatoes skinned, seeded and chopped
1 tablespoon onion grated
1 tablespoon low fat cheese grated
1 tablespoon non fat yoghurt
1 teaspoon mixed dried herbs
black pepper to taste
⅛ teaspoon cayenne pepper
wholemeal breadcrumbs

Put all ingredients except breadcrumbs in a saucepan. Slowly bring to the boil and boil for 1 minute. Remove from heat. Beat in wholemeal breadcrumbs to make a paste consistency. Store in the refrigerator.

Steak paste:

500g topside steak
1 bay leaf
1 tablespoon water
½ teaspoon black pepper
mace and nutmeg ground
¼ teaspoon cayenne pepper

Chop steak into small pieces. Remove all fat. Put all ingredients into a heatproof dish with 1 tablespoon of water. Cover and steam gently for 3 hours. When cool, mince finely in a food processor. Bind with a squeeze of lemon juice. Store in an airtight jar in the refrigerator.

opposite: beef: hot mashed potato; left to right — beef 'stroganoff' (page 40); beef and carrot hotpot (page 39); beef and capsicum (page 37)

overleaf: ice creams: back — pineapple flavoured ice cream on fresh pineapple and kiwi fruit (page 91); fruit salad of orange segments, grapefruit segments, pineapple chunks, passionfruit pulp, orange juice (page 85); front — boysenberry ice cream (page 91); strawberry ice cream over fresh strawberries (page 90)

spinach

spinach and cheese muffins

makes 12

1 cup wholemeal plain flour
1 cup unbleached plain flour
2 teaspoons baking powder
1 teaspoon nutmeg
100g fresh spinach very finely chopped by hand
½ cup low fat grating cheese very finely grated
½ cup evaporated skim milk
½ cup non fat yoghurt
2 tablespoons apple juice concentrate
2 egg whites

Sift dry ingredients twice. Add spinach and cheese and coat lightly with the flour. Combine milk, yoghurt and apple juice concentrate. Add to flour and spinach and mix well. Beat egg whites until stiff peaks form and fold through. Spoon into a lightly greased muffin tray. Cook at 180°C for 25 minutes.

sprouts

These are a vegetable high in vitamin C, a good source of pure protein; they contain natural carbohydrates, vitamins and minerals. They grow in a jar and reach their desired length (between 1–6cm) in 3–5 days.

You can buy commercial sprouters but a jar with a piece of muslin secured over the opening is acceptable.

Choose from a wide variety of seeds, beans and lentils available. Sprout one variety or combine two or more varieties for an added interest in texture and flavour.

Soak the seeds, beans and lentils for 6 hours in luke warm water. Drain. Leave in a light place (not direct sunlight). Rinse sprouts every day and drain well.

Eat them in salads, add to sandwiches, drop them onto soup before serving, use them as a garnish or juice them with other vegetables and fruits. They can be added to any cooked meals before serving, for example casseroles, omelettes.

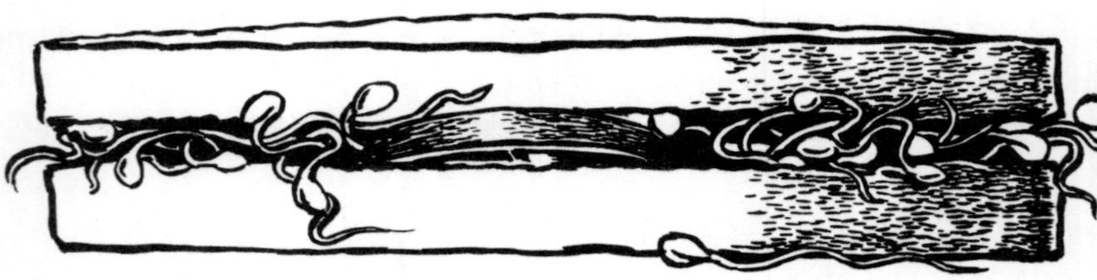

sprouts dagwood

serves 1–2

2 slices salt free wholemeal or grain bread
2 tablespoons mango chutney (see chicken burger *recipe page 60)*
¼–½ cup mung bean or lentil sprouts
2 large slices tomato
4 slices cucumber with skin removed
¼–½ cup alfalfa sprouts
cherry tomatoes

Spread one slice of bread with mango chutney. Spread mung bean or lentil sprouts evenly over the top. Add slices of tomato, cucumber and top with alfalfa sprouts and the second slice of bread.

Thread cherry tomatoes onto a long wooden skewer to the top end. Place skewer through the centre of the sandwich to keep layers in place.

spicy sprouts salad

serves approximately 12

4 celery stalks finely sliced
150g mung bean sprouts
150g lentil sprouts
1 cup sultanas
1 cup unsweetened orange juice
½–1 teaspoon cumin

Soak sultanas in orange juice with cumin for at least 2 hours or overnight. Combine all ingredients and mix well.

strawberries

Strawberries are an excellent source of vitamin C and a fair source of vitamin A and dietary fibre. They include some calcium, phosphorus, iron, potassium, thiamin, riboflavin and niacin, and are low in sodium.

strawberry caterpillar

Use large strawberries to make the caterpillar

Join strawberries together using toothpicks. Break in half if too big and don't forget to remind children that the toothpicks are to be removed before eating!

Decorate the caterpillar's face using long shreds of coconut or thin strips of dried apricot for feelers; sultanas or fresh blueberries for its eyes, and a thin apricot strip or a small sliver of apple for its mouth. The caterpillar can then be placed on a tray and chilled or frozen.

strawberry thickshake

serves 2

1 cup strawberries
2 tablespoons unsweetened orange juice
1 tablespoon apple juice concentrate
2 cups ice cold skim milk

½ cup non fat yoghurt
or
2 tablespoons skim milk powder

Simmer strawberries in orange juice and apple juice until strawberries are soft. Cool. Puree all ingredients and serve.

strawberry and passionfruit topped pavlova

serves 12

1x375ml tin evaporated skim milk well chilled
10 dried apricots
½ cup unsweetened orange juice
1 teaspoon vanilla
1 tablespoon apple juice concentrate
1 teaspoon white wine vinegar
1 tablespoon gelatine
½ cup boiling water
2 cups low fat whipped cream
3 cups strawberries washed and hulled
¼ cup passionfruit pulp

Simmer apricots in orange juice for 10 minutes or until soft. Puree. Beat milk until thick and at least doubled in size. Blend in apricots, vanilla, apple juice concentrate and vinegar. Dissolve gelatine in boiling water and fold into mixture. Pour into a round, springform cheesecake tin. Refrigerate until firm. Top with cream, strawberries and passionfruit pulp.

Variation:
4 cups Mountain Maid apple juice unsweetened
4 teaspoons agar
2 tablespoons apple juice concentrate
2 teaspoons vanilla essence
1½ cups non fat yoghurt

Pour apple juice into a saucepan and add agar. Simmer and stir to dissolve. Add apple juice concentrate and vanilla. Allow to cool slightly. Place in a food blender or processor and process until frothy. Add yoghurt and process a further 2 minutes. Pour into flat mould and refrigerate. Top with strawberries and sliced kiwi fruit, strawberries and other berries such as raspberries, blueberries or loganberries, or strawberries and sliced pineapple.

strawberry custard parfait

serves 6

1 quantity of custard (see banana custard *recipe page* 36*)*
6 cups hulled strawberries

Make up custard and let cool slightly. Cut strawberries into quarters. Alternate layers of strawberries and custard in a parfait glass. Decorate the top with sliced strawberries. Refrigerate when custard has completely set.

strawberry custard tarts

makes 8 small tarts

2 cups strawberries washed and hulled

Pastry:
1 cup wholemeal plain flour
1 cup rolled oats
¼ cup cold compressed oil
2 tablespoons apple juice concentrate
2–4 tablespoons unsweetened orange juice

Lightly grease 8 small foil 8x2cm pie plates. Combine all ingredients for pastry in a food processor. Using the steel blade, process until pastry binds together. Cut pastry into 8 equal pieces and roll out to fit the pie plates. Trim edges and place on a baking tray. Cook at 210°C for 10 minutes. Cool.

Custard:
Use the same ingredients as are used in the recipe for *banana custard* recipe on page *36*) Halve all quantities except orange zest. Cook using the same method and leave to cool slightly.

Pour custard into shells. You should have approximately ¼ cup custard left over for children who love to lick the bowl. Refrigerate. Decorate the tops with fresh strawberries.

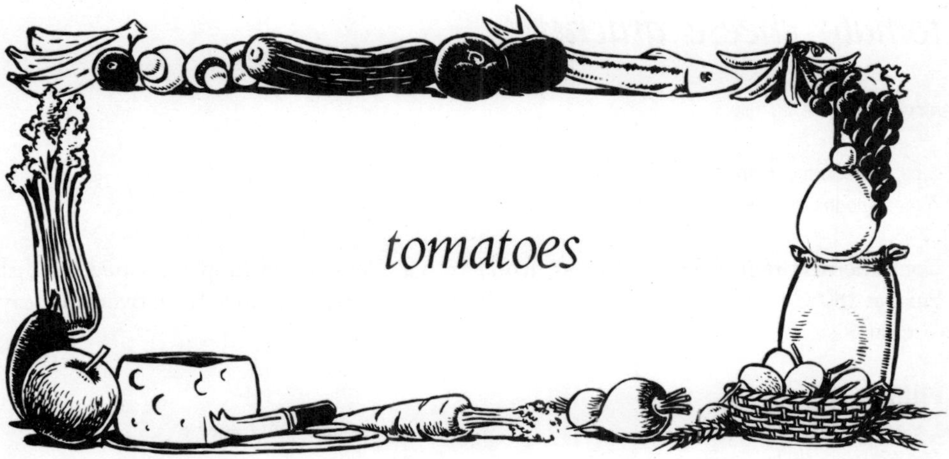

tomatoes

quick and easy tomato soup

serves 4

1 medium sized onion diced
½ teaspoon oregano
½ teaspoon basil
2 celery stalks including green foliage diced
2x425g tins salt free tomatoes
2 tablespoons salt free tomato paste

Cook onion, herbs and celery in a little water until soft (approximately 3 minutes). Puree tomatoes and tomato paste until smooth. Add to the onion and cook gently for 10–15 minutes. Puree again and serve immediately.

Variations:
- Add 1 cup grated raw carrot before serving.
- Add 1 cup finely sliced celery before serving.
- Add 1 cup finely diced mixed red and green capsicum before serving.
- Add ¼ cup fresh chives finely chopped.
- Add 2 teaspoons fresh ginger juice when cooking the onion.
- Add 1 cup potato peeled, diced and cooked before serving.
- Serve chilled tomato soup with non fat yoghurt and a sprinkling of fresh herbs of your choice.

tomato cheese quiche

serves 4–6

3 cups wholemeal breadcrumbs
2 tablespoons salt free tomato juice

Combine base ingredients and press firmly into a 22cm round lightly greased pie dish. Bake at 180°C for 10–15 minutes or until lightly browned. Remove from oven and leave to cool.

Filling:

1 medium sized onion diced
1x425g tin salt free tomatoes
½ teaspoon basil
½ teaspoon oregano
½ teaspoon coriander powder
400g low fat ricotta cheese
4 egg whites
2 large tomatoes
1 cup low fat grating cheese finely grated

Cook onion in a little water until soft (approximately 2–3 minutes). Remove from heat, add tomatoes, basil, oregano, coriander and ricotta cheese. Puree until very smooth. Beat egg whites until light and fluffy and gently fold into tomato mixture. Pour the mixture over the cooked breadcrumb base. Carefully lay slices of tomato on top to cover and spread cheese evenly over the tomato. Cook at 220°C for 15 minutes and turn down to 190°C for a further 30 minutes.

Garnish top with extra slices of tomato and fresh parsley. This quiche is delicious either hot or cold.

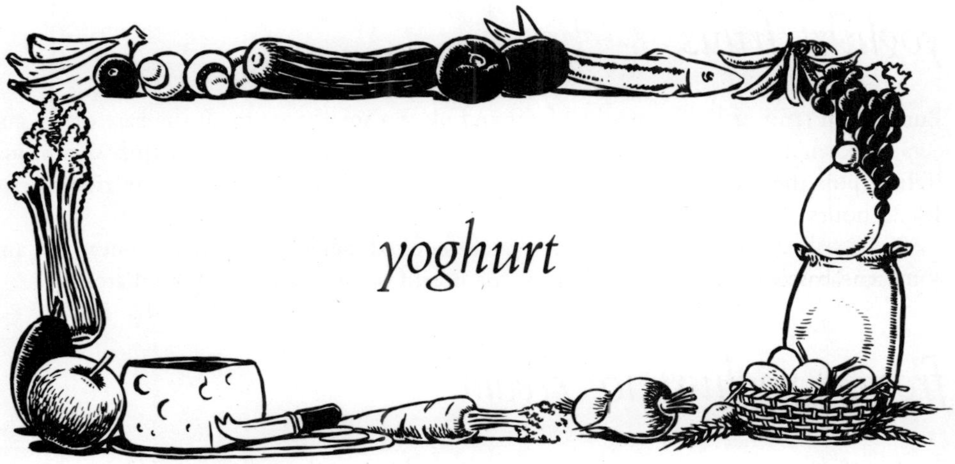

yoghurt

Yoghurt is a cultured milk product in which specific bacteria are added to fresh skim milk to encourage the development of its tangy flavour and custard-like consistency.

Commercial non fat yoghurt is now more readily available, and it has many uses. It is a natural antibiotic as the acid in it helps to kill harmful organisms.

It is easily digested, sometimes more easily than cow's milk, because it is a source of predigested protein. This means that in the process of the fermentation, the protein in yoghurt is partially broken down. Yoghurt helps to balance the bacterial flow in the intestine, especially after illness or after drug therapy. An imbalance of bacterial flora in the intestine can cause diarrhea or flatulence. Yoghurt helps to correct this.

Uses for yoghurt:
The uses for yoghurt are many and it is easily substituted in recipes calling for full cream.

It is a treat in itself or with freshly chopped fruits or crunchy freshly grated vegetables added to it. It can be added to cakes, pastries and dessert pies, and is delicious added to hot or cold soups.

Cooking with yoghurt;
When adding yoghurt to a hot pan remove from heat first and do not bring back to the boil.

If a small amount of flour or cornflour has been added to the cooked dish at the beginning of cooking time, then adding yoghurt should be successful.

Alternatively, add 1–2 tablespoons of cornflour mixed with a little water to approximately 4 cups of yoghurt. Place yoghurt in a food blender or processor and blend until it becomes liquid. Add the cornflour paste and mix well. Heat slowly bringing to a gentle boil. Stir continuously but not vigorously. Reduce heat to barely simmering point and cook, uncovered, for 8 10 minutes or until the sauce has thickened and is quite smooth. The yoghurt can now be added to the cooked foods without the risk of yoghurt curdling.

Non fat yoghurt should be folded through gently rather than stirred through vigorously because the texture of non fat yoghurt separates very easily.

When adding a yoghurt based salad dressing to a salad, always add it to the salad just prior to serving so the yoghurt does not become too watery at the bottom of the salad bowl.

yoghurt fruits

Puree fresh fruit or lightly cooked fruit and place a small amount at the base of a 1 cup ceramic container. Top up with non fat yoghurt. Then, using a long thin spoon, just lightly pull the fruit up through the centre of the yoghurt. Cover and refrigerate for 12–25 hours.

Try mashed banana with lemon juice, cooked apple or apricot, pineapple and combinations of berries. It is delicious for breakfast or as an after school treat.

frozen yoghurt ice cream

3 cups non fat yoghurt
2 tablespoons apple juice concentrate
1–2 teaspoons vanilla essence

Combine all ingredients. Pour into an ice cream maker and follow freezing instructions.

Without ice cream maker:
Pour into a stainless steel bowl and place in freezer. As yoghurt freezes around the edge of the bowl, stir the frozen particles into the mixture. Continue to do this until all yoghurt is frozen.

It should be served more as a soft serve dessert than a hard ice cream. Do not beat the yoghurt as the texture will easily separate.

summer cucumber yoghurt soup

serves 6

2 large cucumbers
2 cups non fat yoghurt
½ cup skim milk
2 tablespoons chives or spring onions finely chopped
2 teaspoon fresh dill finely chopped
1 jonathon apple

Peel cucumbers and cut in half. Remove seeds and grate. Combine remaining ingredients and mix well. Chill for several hours so that flavour can develop. Garnish with thin slices of apple.

peach yoghurt mousse

1x825g tin peaches unsweetened and drained
2 tablespoons apple juice concentrate
½ teaspoon orange essence
1 tablespoon gelatine
3 tablespoons boiling water
1½–2 cups non fat yoghurt

Blend peaches, apple juice concentrate and orange essence. Dissolve gelatine in boiling water and add to peach mixture. Fold in the yoghurt. Pour into a wet mould and refrigerate until set. Serve with fresh strawberries and slices of fresh peaches.

frozen yoghurt popsicles

Strawberry:

1 cup fresh strawberries mashed
1–2 tablespoons apple juice concentrate (optional)
¼ teaspoon orange essence
2 cups non fat yoghurt

Mix all ingredients thoroughly and spoon into icypole moulds.

Banana:

1 cup mashed bananas
1 tablespoon lemon juice
1 teaspoon vanilla essence
2 cups non fat yoghurt

As above.

Passionfruit yoghurt:

2 cups non fat yoghurt
¼ cup passionfruit pulp

As above.

Pineapple crunch yoghurt:

1 tablespoon lemon juice
or
½ teaspoon orange essence
2 cups non fat yoghurt
1 cup unsweetened crushed pineapple

As above.

Carob peppermint:

1 tablespoon carob powder
1 tablespoon boiling water
½ teaspoon peppermint essence
½ teaspoon vanilla essence
1 tablespoon apple juice concentrate
2 cups non fat yoghurt

Combine carob powder and boiling water to dissolve carob. Mix all ingredients thoroughly and pour into icypole moulds.

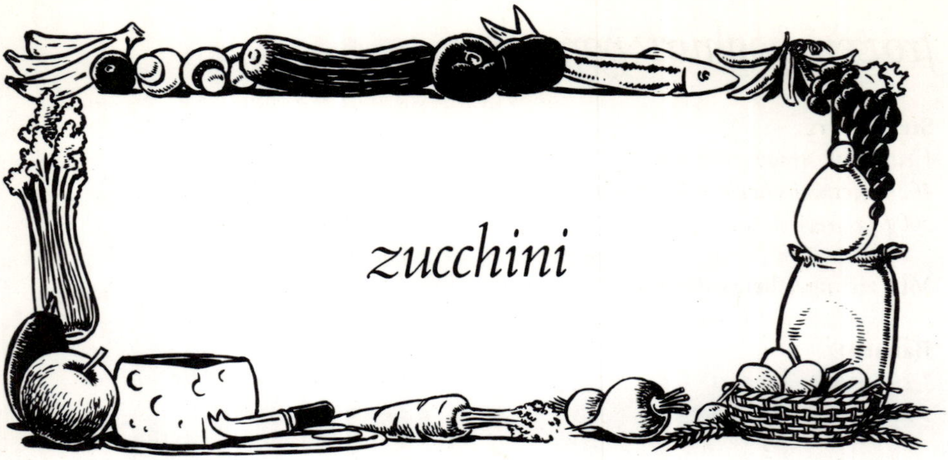

zucchini moussaka

serves 6-8

600g large zucchini cut into thin slices
1 onion finely diced
2 cloves garlic crushed
250g carrots finely diced
250g mushrooms finely diced
3 bay leaves
1 teaspoon oregano
1 teaspoon basil
2x400g tins salt free tomatoes and juice
¼ cup salt free tomato paste

Cook zucchini until just tender and drain. Cook onion and garlic in 2 tablespoons water until soft and transparent. Add remaining ingredients except tomato paste and simmer, covered, for 15 minutes. Remove bay leaves and chop up tomatoes using a wooden spoon. Add tomato paste. Turn heat up and cook, uncovered, until sauce thickens. stirring occasionally.

White Sauce:
500ml soy milk or skim milk or evaporated skim milk
4 tablespoons cornflour
dash of cayenne pepper
1 tablespoon skim milk herb cheese
1 cup grated low fat grating cheese grated

Place soy milk in saucepan, reserving ¼ cup. Blend ¼ cup soy milk with cornflour to make a paste. Bring milk to almost boiling and stir in cayenne pepper and skim milk herb cheese. Add cornflour and stir continuously until sauce thickens.

Lightly grease an oblong ovenproof dish with high sides. Place a layer of zucchini on the base of the dish. Pour over a layer of sauce, enough to spread and cover zucchini. Repeat with alternate layers of zucchini and sauce. Top with layer of white sauce. Sprinkle over cheese. Cook at 190°C for 20-30 minutes or until cheese has melted and is brown and bubbling.

zucchini meatloaf

serves 10–12

400g zucchini grated
500g fat free minced beef (rump)
1 medium sized onion finely chopped
100g red capsicum finely chopped
2 cups wholemeal breadcrumbs
1 egg white
2 tablespoons salt free tomato paste
1 tablespoon fresh tarragon or parsley finely chopped
1 tablespoon fresh basil finely chopped
ground black pepper to taste (optional)
¼ cup low fat grating cheese grated

Combine all ingredients except cheese. Using hands mix all ingredients thoroughly. Press mixture into a foil lined terrine dish. Press down firmly and cover with foil. Place terrine in a large pan of water so that the water reaches at least 2cm up the side of the terrine dish. Cook at 180°C for 1¼ hours.

Drain off any liquid and unmould terrine onto a foil lined baking tray. Sprinkle over cheese. Return to oven and cook a further 10 minutes. Let stand 10 minutes before slicing if serving hot, or cool and refrigerate.

Serve as a meat luncheon loaf with salads or use in sandwiches or on wholemeal biscuits.

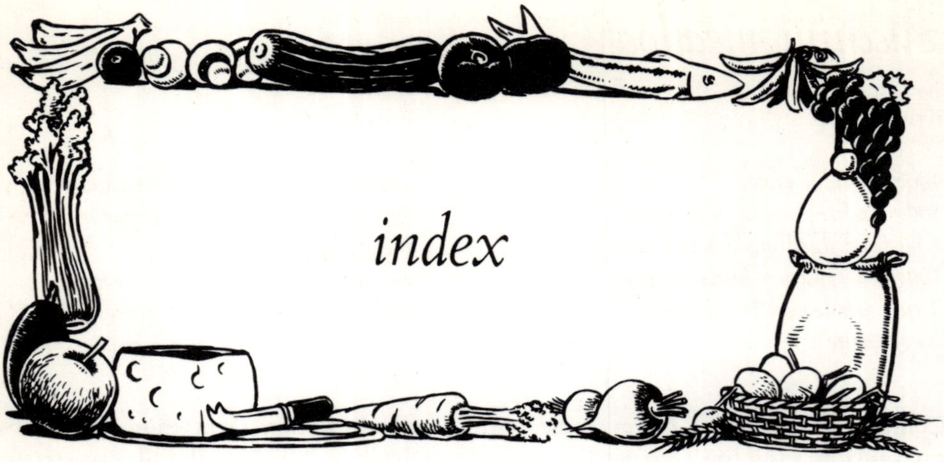

index